STATE OF THE ART PROGRAM

Portfolios

(Level 4)

Pupil's Edition

Robyn Montana Turner

BK
Educating tomorrow today

BARRETT KENDALL PUBLISHING, Ltd.
AUSTIN, TEXAS

CREDITS

EDITORIAL

Project Director: *Linda Dunlap*

Senior Development Editor: *Linda Dunlap*

Editors: *Melissa Blackwell Burke, Claire Miller Colombo, Kathleen Fitzgibbon, Jody Frank, Mary Ann Frishman, Patty Moynahan, Tara Turner, Anne Walker*

Copy Editors: *Kathleen Unger, Sandra Wolfgang*

Editorial Support: *Mary Corbett, Elaine Clift Gore, Judy McBurney*

Administrative Manager: *Mark Blangger*

Administrative Support: *Laurie O'Meara*

DESIGN, PRODUCTION, AND PHOTO RESEARCH

Project Director: *Pun Nio*

Designers: *Leslie Kell Designs, Jane Thurmond Designs, Pun Nio*

Design and Electronic Files: *Dodson Publication Services, Leslie Kell Designs, Jane Thurmond Designs, Linda Kensicki*

Photo Research: *Mark Blangger, Laurie O'Meara*

Photo Art Direction: *Jodie Baker, Andrew Yates Photography*

Cover Design: *Leslie Kell Designs*

Printed in the United States of America

ISBN 1-889105-16-3   1 2 3 4 5 6 7   VH 02 01 00 99 98 97 96

STATE OF THE ART PROGRAM

Portfolios

Consultants

Doug Blandy, Ph.D.
Associate Professor
> Program in Arts and Administration
> University of Oregon
> Eugene, Oregon

Cindy G. Broderick, Ph.D.
Art Faculty
> Alamo Heights Junior School
> Alamo Heights Independent
>   School District
> San Antonio, Texas

Sara Chapman, M.A.
Visual Arts Coordinator
> Alief Independent School District
> Houston, Texas

Brenda J. Chappell, Ph.D.
Art Consultant
> Multicultural Curriculum and Women
> Artists
> Columbus, Ohio

James Clarke, M.A.
*Program Director for Visual Arts and
Elementary Creative Drama*
> Aldine Independent School District
> Houston, Texas

Georgia Collins, Ph.D.
Professor, Department of Art
> University of Kentucky
> Lexington, Kentucky

Gloria Contreras, Ph.D.
*Professor, Department of Teacher
Education and Administration*
> University of North Texas
> Denton, Texas

Sandra M. Epps, Ph.D.
Director, Multicultural Programs
> Community School District Five
> New York, New York

Diane C. Gregory, Ph.D.
*Associate Professor of Art Education,
Department of Art and Design*
> Southwest Texas State University
> San Marcos, Texas

Susan M. Mayer, M.A.
*Coordinator of Museum Education,
Senior Lecturer of Art*
> The University of Texas at Austin
> Austin, Texas

Aaronetta Hamilton Pierce
Consultant
> African American Art and Artists
> San Antonio, Texas

Renee Sandell, Ph.D.
Professor, Department of Art Education
> Maryland Institute, College of Art
> Baltimore, Maryland

Contributing Writers

Pamela Geiger Stephens, Ph.D
Art Education Consultant
Colleyville, Texas

Sharon Warwick, M.Ed., M.S.A.
Art Specialist
Central Junior High School
Euless, Texas
Tarrant County Junior College
Hurst, Texas

Kay K. Wilson, M.A.
Art Specialist
North Texas Institute for
Educators on the Visual Arts
University of North Texas
Denton, Texas

Reviewers

Gini Robertson-Baker
Classroom Teacher
Bivins Elementary School
Amarillo Independent School District
Amarillo, Texas

Rosalinda Champion
Art Specialist
Edinburg Senior High School
Edinburg Consolidated School District
Edinburg, Texas

Susan Daniel
Classroom Teacher
Mary Bryan Elementary School
M.S.D. of Perry Township
Indianapolis, Indiana

Barbara Louisot
Art Specialist
Tedder Elementary School
Broward County Schools
Pompano Beach, Florida

Nancy Mayeda
Principal
Creative Fine Arts Magnet School
San Francisco Unified School District
San Francisco, California

Barbara Kimmel-Palmer
Art Specialist
Yorbita Elementary School
Rowland Unified School District
La Puente, California

Bonnie Schry
Art Specialist
Boca Raton Christian School
Boca Raton, Florida

Jamie M. Woods
Art Specialist
Edgewater Elementary School
Anne Arundel County Schools
Edgewater, Maryland

Marilyn Wylie
Art Specialist
Bethune Academy
Aldine Independent School District
Houston, Texas

CONTENTS

Andrew Wyeth. (Detail) *Christina's World,* 1948. Tempera on gessoed panel, 32¼ by 47¾ inches. The Museum of Modern Art, New York. Purchase. Photograph © 1996 The Museum of Modern Art, New York.

Art and Your World

What if someone asked you, "What is art?" How would you answer that question? Some say art is anything that shows or tells about ideas, experiences, or feelings. Others say it's expression. Still others say no one can define art.

Art doesn't have to be defined or understood to be enjoyed. Just like everyday life, art can simply be experienced. Yet the more you understand what art can offer, the richer your experience of it will be.

This unit may help you understand some of the things that art can offer. It introduces a few of the many ways that artists see their world. One way that artists observe is by studying **elements of art** and **principles of design.**

Elements are to an artist what words are to a writer. Elements are the parts of an artwork. Principles are to an artist what sentences and paragraphs are to a writer. Principles are the guides artists use to arrange elements in an artwork. Elements and principles help artists communicate through a visual language.

Elements

- line
- shape
- color
- value
- texture
- form
- space

Principles

- unity
- variety
- emphasis
- balance
- proportion
- pattern
- rhythm

First Look

What is the title of the painting?
What do you suppose the title means?
How does the painting make you feel?

Ways of Seeing

A

Has anyone ever said that you see the world through rose-colored glasses? This expression means that you have a positive attitude toward life. Everyone sees the world in a different way. Each person's vision is special.

Artists young and old have expressed ways they see their world. Some have even created pictures of themselves viewing the world. You can see **self-portraits** in **B**, **C**, **D**, and **E**.

B Elizabeth Layton (American, born 1909). *Self-Portrait Holding Rose with Thorns,* 1985. Pastel with pencil on paper, 18 by 7 inches. The National Museum of Women in the Arts. Gift of Wallace and Wilhelmina Holladay.

Artists have their own **styles,** or special ways of creating artworks. Notice the different styles of the self-portraits. What do you think the artists were saying about themselves?

 Pieter Brueghel, the Elder. *Painter and the Patron (with Brueghel's self-portrait),* ca. 1566. Pen and ink drawing, 8⅔ by 10¼ inches. Graphische Sammlung Albertina, Vienna, Austria. Photograph by Erich Lessing/Art Resource, New York.

 Violeta, Loma Park Elementary. *Purple Hat.* Tempera and crayon on paper, 12 by 18 inches.

Seeing, Planning, Thinking Like an Artist

Do you have a special style of drawing?
Draw a self-portrait.
Show yourself viewing the world around you.

E Molly, Heflin Elementary. *Self-Portrait.* Crayon and markers on paper, 11 by 17 inches.

A

B

Sketchbooks and Portfolios

Many artists draw **sketches** to help them explore what they see or remember. Sketches can express imaginative ideas. They can become plans for future artworks.

Perhaps you've kept a collection of your sketches. Keeping a **sketchbook** can help you organize your sketches. It can become a record of what you see, think, or imagine. Some of your sketches may give you ideas for making artworks.

Portfolios help artists organize a collection of their own artworks. Artists can look at their portfolios to see both problems and progress in their work. They can discover ways to improve their skills and future artworks.

Try Your Hand
Making a Sketchbook and Portfolio
Look on pages 139 and 140 to help you. The sketchbook can be about the size of this book. The portfolio will be larger.

How will your sketchbook help you during the school year?

What can you learn about your artwork by keeping a portfolio?

Ways of Seeing   5

A World of Lines and Shapes

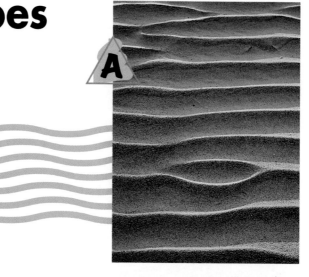

Look around your world. It is filled with lines and shapes.

Lines in artworks show directions. These directions send visual messages. They often remind people of certain feelings.

Lines can be **horizontal** ≡, as in **A**. Horizontal lines often remind people of calm, quiet feelings. Lines can be **vertical** ‖‖‖, as in **B**. Vertical lines can suggest feelings of strength in things that reach up. Lines can also be **diagonal** ⫽⫽, as in **C**. Diagonal lines suggest activity. People sometimes feel nervous or active when they look at diagonal lines.

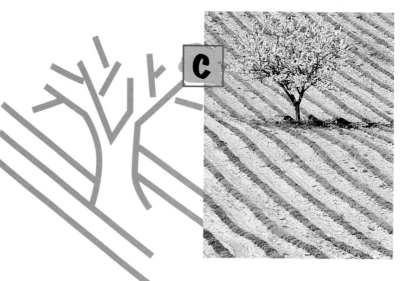

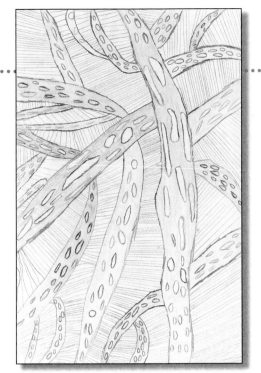

 D Frankie, Smith Elementary. *Dried Cactus Enlargement.* Pencil on paper, 18 by 12 inches.

 E Christopher, Liestman Elementary. *Symbols in Space.* Tempera and crayon on sponge-painted paper, 18 by 12 inches.

F

The buildings in **B** show a human-made environment. The shapes, such as squares and rectangles, are **geometric.** Name some other geometric shapes you've learned about.

Now look at the **organic** tree shape in **C.** Organic shapes have uneven curves. Examples are hills and rivers in the natural environment. Using your finger in the air, draw some organic shapes.

Seeing, Planning, Thinking Like an Artist

Make a sketch. Use horizontal, vertical, and diagonal lines.
Include both geometric and organic shapes.

Clara McDonald Williamson. *The Old Chisholm Trail,* 1952. Oil on panel, 24 by 36½ inches. The Roland P. Murdock Collection, Wichita Art Museum, Wichita, Kansas.

Communicating Through Line, Shape, and Space

Artists communicate through visual language. They send messages without words.

The artist of **A** used horizontal and vertical lines to communicate a peaceful feeling. Some are **actual** lines. You can see these lines. Others are **implied** lines. You see these lines, even though they're not drawn or painted as actual lines.

Find an implied vertical line made by the herd of cattle. Point to implied horizontal lines made by distant trees and hills.

Notice how your eye starts at the **foreground.** Then it travels to the **middle ground** and on to the **background.** The artist made shapes look near to you or far away. Many of the cattle shapes **overlap** in front of one another, to help show distance. Study the outlines in **B** to see overlapping.

Illustration of shapes that overlap in A.

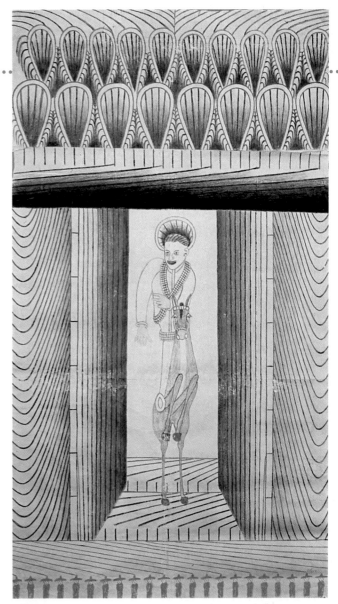

Now look at **C**. Are the horse and rider in the foreground, middle ground, or background? Where did the artist use horizontal, vertical, and diagonal lines? How do those lines make you feel? Are they actual or implied lines? Read the **credit line** for **C**. Are you surprised to learn that the artist drew on a paper sack?

A closed space can make you feel boxed in. Which artwork shows a closed space? Which artist created an open space? How does the open space make you feel?

C Martin Ramirez. *Untitled (Horse and Rider)*, 1954. Pencil, tempera, and crayon on collaged paper, 35 by 58¾ inches. Collection of Jim Nutt and Gladys Nilsson. Photograph courtesy of the Phyllis Kind Gallery, New York.

Try Your Hand
Drawing on a Paper Sack

1. Draw a cowgirl or cowboy on a paper sack.
2. Use a dark crayon to plan your foreground, middle ground, and background.

How can you use line direction to help communicate ideas and feelings? Will you show an open or a closed space?

A World of Spaces

Doan, Liestman Elementary. *Positive/Negative Leaves.* Marker on paper, 11 by 17 inches.

Andy, Randolph Field Elementary. *Spotted-Faced Cat.* Tempera on paper, 18 by 12 inches.

People see spaces in artworks in different ways. In **A**, most people see the dark shapes first. These areas are called **positive space.** The area around the positive space is called **negative space.** Negative space serves as contrast. It helps you see the positive space. Both positive and negative space are parts of the **composition,** or the whole artwork.

Positive space has outlines, edges, or colors that attract your eye. Point to the positive space in **B**. Why did your eye go to that space first? Where is the negative space?

Jasper Johns. *Cups 4 Picasso,* 1972. Lithograph, printed in color, composition: 14⅛ by 32¼ inches. The Museum of Modern Art, New York. Gift of Celeste Bartos. © 1998 Jasper Johns/Licensed by VAGA, New York, NY. Photograph © 1996 The Museum of Modern Art, New York.

The artist of **C** planned this composition to be a visual puzzle. In fact, he wanted to confuse the viewer. Look at the artwork once. Then squint your eyes to look at it again. What do you see? Which is the positive space? Which is the negative space?

Seeing, Planning, Thinking Like an Artist

Plan a composition for the cover of a compact disc or a CD-ROM.
Show contrast between positive and negative space.
Place dark shapes next to light ones.
Will you use colors or black and white?

A World of Spaces 11

Rosa Bonheur. *Plowing in the Nivernais (Labourage Nivernais),* 1849. Oil on canvas, approximately 53½ by 104 inches. Musee d'Orsay. Photograph © R.M.N.-Gérard Blot.

Ways of Expressing with Lines, Shapes, and Spaces

Artists have different ways of expressing what they see. Two artists may show the same **subject,** such as a person or an animal. Yet they may have completely different styles. The subjects of **A** through **F** are cows. However, the styles are not the same. Look carefully.

The artist of **A** painted in France about 100 years ago. She used a **realistic** style, called **Realism.** She made her subjects look lifelike. Some say the plowed soil looks so real you could reach out and pick up a clump of it. Notice the shadows on the soil.

Point out shadows beneath the cattle. Shadows help make flat areas appear full and lifelike.

Details such as **B** are small parts of a larger artwork. Sometimes they are enlarged. Then you can see the small part close up.

Rosa Bonheur. (Detail) *Plowing in the Nivernais (Labourage Nivernais),* 1849. Oil on canvas, approximately 53½ by 104 inches. Musee d'Orsay. Photograph © R.M.N.-Gérard Blot.

Theo van Doesburg (C.E.M. Küpper). Study for Composition (The Cow), 1916. Pencil drawing, 4⅝ by 6¼ inches. The Museum of Modern Art, New York. Purchase. Photograph © 1996 The Museum of Modern Art, New York.

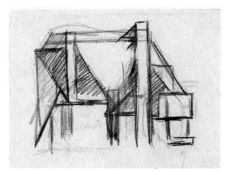

Theo van Doesburg (C.E.M. Küpper). Study for *Composition (The Cow)*, 1916. Pencil drawing, 4⅝ by 6¼ inches. The Museum of Modern Art, New York. Purchase. Photograph © 1996 The Museum of Modern Art, New York.

Theo van Doesburg (C.E.M. Küpper). *Composition (The Cow)*, ca. 1917. Oil on canvas, 14¾ by 25 inches. The Museum of Modern Art, New York. Purchase. Photograph © 1996 The Museum of Art, New York.

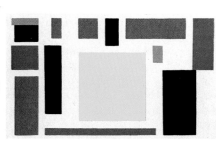

Theo van Doesburg (C.E.M. Küpper). *Composition (The Cow)*, ca. 1917, dated 1916. Tempera, oil, and charcoal on paper, 15⅝ by 22¾ inches. The Museum of Modern Art, New York. Purchase. Photograph © 1996 The Museum of Modern Art, New York.

The artist of **C**, **D**, **E**, and **F** showed how a realistic style can change to become an **abstract** one. Starting with the realistic design in **C**, the artist added to and took away elements to make **D**, **E**, and **F**. Follow those changes from **C** through **F**. How did the artist change line, shape, space, and color to create an abstract design?

Casey, Woodridge Elementary. *Home on the Range.* Tempera on paper, 12 by 18 inches.

 Try Your Hand

Creating an Abstract Artwork

1. Draw a realistic subject such as a horse or another animal.
2. Use oil pastels or paints to make an abstract artwork that shows at least one change from your realistic design.

How will you add or take away elements from your realistic design?
How many changes will you choose to make?

13

ARTIST AT WORK

Andrew Wyeth

(AN-droo WY-uhth)

(1917–   )

James Wyeth. *Portrait of Andrew Wyeth,* 1969. Oil on canvas, 24 by 32 inches. Collection of the artist. © 1998 James Wyeth.

Andrew Wyeth is part of a family of American artists. His father, N. C. Wyeth, was a well-known painter. Two of his sisters, Carolyn and Henriette, became artists. His son James is also a painter.

As a boy, Wyeth had a lively imagination. He began to draw when he was a child. He often brought his daydreams to life through his pictures. When he was older, he studied art with his father. His father was proud of Andrew's work. By the age of 20, Andrew Wyeth was already selling his pictures.

Year after year, Wyeth has painted images of people and places familiar to him. He paints pictures of the Pennsylvania farmland where he grew up and still lives. And he paints pictures of the Maine coast, where he spends part of each year. He shows the changing faces of his neighbors, their houses, and the land that surrounds them.

Wyeth's paintings are like photographs with something extra added. He paints things the way they look. But the painted scenes are never exactly the same as the real ones. Wyeth adds something of what he sees in his daydreams.

WRITE ABOUT ART

Look at *Christina's World*. Andrew Wyeth painted many pictures of his friend Christina Olson. This picture was her favorite.

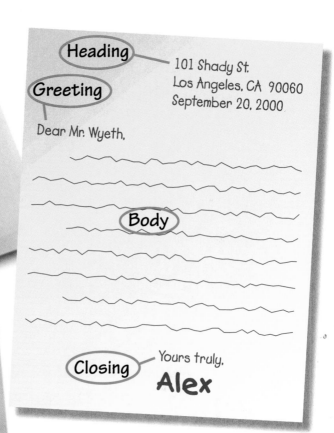

Write Away

Pretend you are writing a letter to Wyeth. What would you say to the artist about his painting? What questions would you ask him?

Use these ideas or your own to help you think of what to say in the letter.

Things to say in my letter:
• Questions about the artist and the scene he painted
• What I think about Christina
• How the painting makes me feel
• What I like best about the painting

Heading

101 Shady St.
Los Angeles, CA 90060
September 20, 2000

Greeting

Dear Mr. Wyeth,

Body

Closing

Yours truly,
Alex

A Word About
Christina's World

Christina Olson was the artist's neighbor in Maine. She was unable to walk. This painting shows her in a field near her house. The artist observed her there one day. The painting is an expression of his admiration for her strength and courage.

TALK ABOUT ART

 Andrew Wyeth. *Christina's World*, 1948. Tempera on gessoed panel, 32¼ by 47¾ inches. The Museum of Modern Art, New York. Purchase. Photograph © 1996 The Museum of Modern Art, New York.

Look at A to answer these questions:

1. What do you see? Describe the lines, shapes, textures, and colors you see. Point to an area defined by an implied line. Describe the open space in the painting. Which shapes represent positive space? negative space? Point to areas where the artist used shadows.

2. How is *Christina's World* arranged? Explain which style Wyeth used. Tell why you think so. Discuss his use of foreground, middle ground, and background. How did he make Christina the most important part of the painting?

3. What does *Christina's World* mean? Does the lighter area in the field have special meaning? Why do you think the artist shows Christina leaning toward the house? How does this painting remind you of your feelings about your own world? How do you think the artist feels about his neighbor and her world?

Philip Evergood. (Detail) *Her World,* 1948. Oil on canvas, 48 by 35⅝ inches. The Metropolitan Museum of Art, Arthur Hoppock Hearn Fund, 1950 (50.29). Photograph © 1986 The Metropolitan Museum of Art.

4. What's your opinion? What is special about **A**? Do you know someone who might enjoy seeing *Christina's World*? Explain. How would it feel to visit this place in Maine? Have your feelings about this painting changed since you first saw it? Tell why or why not.

Compare A and B.

Compare the worlds in **A** and **B**. How do the sky and ground differ in the paintings? Explain how both worlds appear alike and different.

A Word About
Her World

This painting shows a rural scene in the United States. The artist placed his subject behind a fence in the foreground. The group of houses form an implied line in the middle ground. What might this person be thinking about?

PORTFOLIO PROJECT

Animals in the Art World

What might an animal's world be like?
Use your imagination and art tools to find out.

1. Color many shapes with light colors of crayons. Press hard and fill the whole paper.

2. Color over the paper again with a black crayon. Press hard.

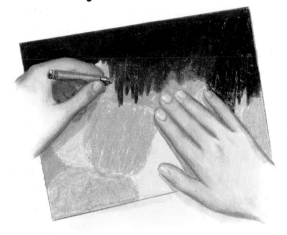

3. Use a toothpick to draw your animal and its world. Include a foreground, middle ground, and background.

4. Use a craftstick and other tools to scratch away the negative space.

How did you scratch away negative space to show details?
Does the space in your animal's world look open or closed?
How would it feel to visit there?

PORTFOLIO GALLERY

Freddie, Hogg Elementary.
Swan. Crayon and sequins
on paper, 12 by 9½ inches.

David, Hogg Elementary.
Eagle. Crayon on paper,
9 by 12 inches.

What Have You Learned?

Sketchbook Progress

1. Why is it important to include details in a self-portrait?

2. Look at your drawing that uses different shapes and lines. What kind of shape did you draw the most? What line direction did you use the most? Give your drawing a title that tells about the mood.

3. Look at your design for a compact disc or CD-ROM cover. What space do you see first in your design? Where have you used negative space in your design? Why is contrast important to your design?

Portfolio Progress

Try Your Hand

4. How will a sketchbook be helpful to you? Your portfolio will be helpful to you also. How do you plan to use it to improve your work?

5. How did you show overlapping in your paper-sack drawing?

6. Describe the details you drew to make your animal appear realistic. Describe the changes you made. Is your second artwork abstract or realistic?

Portfolio Project

7. Describe the details about the animals.

8. How did you show the textures of the animals, plants, and other objects?

9. Would you describe your drawing as realistic or abstract?

10. List three or more things you like about your finished work.

Unit Review

Doris, Boone Elementary. *All the Comforts of Home.* Watercolor, marker on paper, 8½ by 11 inches.

1. What elements of art are used in the artwork above?

2. What principles of design do you see? Describe what is in the foreground, middle ground, and background.

3. Does the artwork on this page show mostly actual lines or implied lines? Point out some examples.

4. Is this artwork made in a realistic style or an abstract style? Explain.

5. List two elements of art. Write a definition for each one. Use your own words.

6. List two principles of design. Write a definition for each one.

Jaune Quick-to-See Smith. *Family Tree,* 1986. Pastel on paper, 30 by 22 inches. Collection of Bernice and Harold Steinbaum. Courtesy of Steinbaum Krauss Gallery, New York.

Art as a Cultural Record

The earth is a planet of many cultures. Continents, countries, states, cities—even small towns—all have different cultures. Every culture carries with it a story of its own rich history. That story tells about the ideas, beliefs, and values of the people who share the culture.

Artists make visual records of these cultures. Their artworks describe customs, or ways of doing things. They show ideas about shelter, clothing, religion, and other things that make a culture special.

Have you ever thought about what people who live in the year 2999 might discover about your culture? Today's artists will leave a visual record of it. Which parts of your culture do you think are important? How would you record them visually?

First Look

What do you see in this drawing?
Does it show a real or an imaginary scene? Explain.
How does the drawing make you feel?

Recording with Color

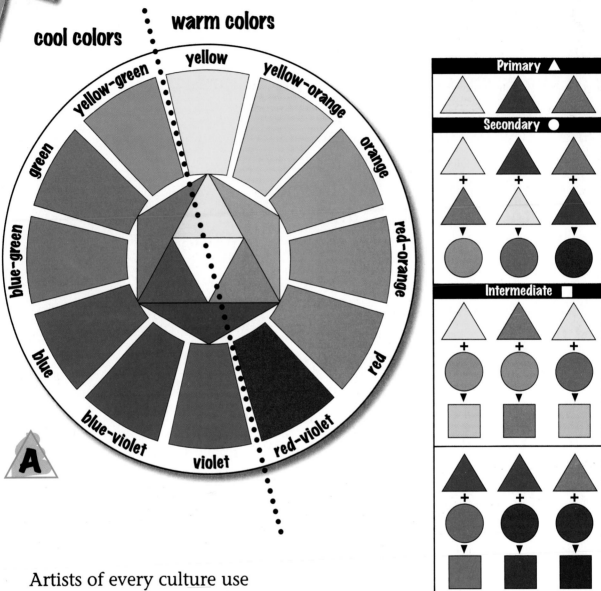

cool colors

warm colors

A

Primary ▲

Secondary ●

Intermediate ■

Artists of every culture use color to express their thoughts and feelings. As an artist, you've learned a lot about color. For example, the name of a color is its **hue.** What hues do you see in the color wheel in **A**?

Take some time to review the different hues in **A**. You may recall that the **primary colors**

are yellow, **red,** and **blue.** Mix two primary colors and you get a **secondary color. Orange, violet,** and **green** are secondary colors. To get an **intermediate color,** you mix a primary color with a secondary color.

 Richard, Hoelscher Elementary. *Landscape Abstract.* Tempera on paper, approximately 17 by 14 inches.

 Joey, Winston Elementary. *Untitled.* Tempera on paper, 18 by 12 inches.

Notice that the color wheel in **A** is divided into halves. It shows **warm colors** and **cool colors.** Artists use these and other **color schemes** to create special moods. Warm colors can show excitement, anger, or love. Cool colors often show loneliness, sadness, or peaceful feelings.

Now look for other color schemes. **Analogous colors** are next to each other on the color wheel. For example, **blue-green**, **green**, and **yellow-green** are analogous colors. Point out some others that you like. **Complementary colors** are opposite each other on the color wheel. **Blue** and **orange** are complementary colors. How many pairs of complementary colors can you find?

Seeing, Planning, Thinking Like an Artist

Experiment with hues.
Use markers. Show three color schemes.
Use tempera paints. Practice mixing colors to get secondary and intermediate hues.
What do these hues and color schemes make you think of?

Recording with Color 25

View of Murnau, Germany, showing church.

Wassily Kandinsky. *Murnau with Church I (Murnau mit Kirche I),* 1910. Oil and watercolor on cardboard, 25½ by 19¾ inches. Städtische Galerie im Lenbachhaus, Munich. Photograph © AKG London.

Visual Records of Landmarks

Artists often use color to show landmarks, or places that many people know about. Look at **B** and **C**. Then read the titles. Are you surprised to learn that the subject of both paintings is a church? The artists who painted these images used different styles. Each one had a special way of using colors, lines, and shapes to show ideas.

The artist of **B** painted with other artists in a German village. They became known as German **Expressionists.** Their style expressed a mood or a feeling.

They often painted a **fantasy,** or dreamlike, scene. Compare **B** with the photograph of the same village in **A**. Point to shapes that are the same in both. Locate the foreground, middle ground, and background of each one.

Notice the different **color values** of light and dark colors in **B**. The artist made each light value, or **tint,** by adding a color to white. He made each dark value, or **shade,** by adding black to a color. The **contrast** of dark values against light ones helps you see the shapes.

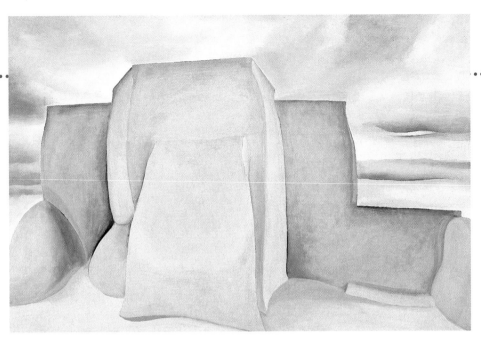

Georgia O'Keeffe. *Ranchos Church–Taos*, 1930. Oil on canvas, 24¼ by 36 inches. Courtesy of Amon Carter Museum, Ft. Worth, Texas. © 1997 The Georgia O'Keeffe Foundation/Artists Rights Society (ARS), New York.

The artist of **C** created this painting of an adobe church in New Mexico. The artist was inspired by the back **view** of the church shown in **E**. Many colors in **C**, **D**, and **E** are **neutral colors.** Black, white, and gray are the neutral colors. Artists also use tints and shades of brown as neutrals.

Try Your Hand

Creating a Two-Part Painting of a Community Landmark

1. On one half of a large paper, paint a fantasy scene showing the landmark. Use the hues on the color wheel. Mix tints and shades.
2. On the other half, paint the same landmark. Use neutral colors. Show a realistic scene.

How do your two views compare with each other?

What does your landmark tell about your culture?

Recording with Color   **27**

Lesson 5

Exploring Balance and Pattern

Artists know that **balance** is an important part of every artwork. They work with three basic types of balance: symmetrical, radial, and asymmetrical.

The artwork in **A** shows **symmetrical balance.** Both sides are about the same. Now look at the round window in **B**. It shows **radial balance.** Lines, shapes, and colors are visually connected to a center point. They are repeated to create **patterns.** These stained-glass windows are made of pieces of colored glass. An artist designed them for a church. It was built in France nearly 800 years ago. When light shines through the **transparent** glass, it sparkles with colors.

The structure in **C** shows **asymmetrical balance.** Parts on each side are not the same, yet the composition looks and feels balanced. This landmark church rests in the mountains of Mexico.

A

Vanessa, Pfeiffer Elementary. *Beautiful Batik.* Resist medium on fabric, 15 by 12 inches.

B

Artist unknown. (Detail) *Rose de France,* ca. 1200. Stained-glass window, Chartres Cathedral, Chartres, France. Photograph © Adam Woolfit/Robert Harding Picture Library.

 Cathedral in Valenciana, Mexico.

D

Amber, Bethune Academy. *Stained-Glass Window.* Construction paper and tissue paper, diameter 10 inches.

Try Your Hand

Designing Your Own Stained-Glass Window

1. Cut a large circle of black construction paper.
2. Fold the circle in half, then in half again, and once more.
3. Snip off the tip. Cut out small shapes along the fold. Open the circle.
4. With a paintbrush, spread thin glue over it.
5. Cut the tissue paper and arrange it over the holes. Then brush thin glue all over the circle again.

Hang the circle in the window to dazzle your eyes!

Exploring Balance and Pattern 29

Dr. John Biggers. *25th Precinct, 3rd Ward: Houston,* 1984. Mixed media, 42 by 50 inches. Photograph courtesy of Earlie Hudnall.

Visual Records of Strength

All cultures have visual **symbols** to represent ideas and values. For example, a heart shape can be a symbol of love. The artworks on these pages show some cultural symbols of strength.

Sometimes artists use lines to help them express the **theme,** or overall idea, in an artwork. Vertical lines can express a theme of strength. Lines can also show feelings. For example, horizontal lines often show calmness, and diagonal lines might show tension.

The artist of **A** painted images of homes called shotgun houses. A shotgun house is long and narrow. Each room is behind another. Discuss the artist's use of horizontal, vertical, and diagonal lines. How did he make the women appear strong? What does each woman hold in her hands? What might this symbolize?

Discuss the balance in **A**. How many patterns can you find? Point to tints and shades. What do you think the birds symbolize?

Now look at **B**. Discuss this artist's use of vertical lines. How does the artist use foreground, middle ground, and background?

In both **A** and **B**, find textures that are rough, smooth, hard, soft, silky, or bumpy. These **tactile textures** look as if you could feel them. Now find **visual textures**, or textures you can see. These textures might be shiny or dull.

B Grant Wood. *American Gothic,* 1930. Oil on beaver board, 29¾ by 25 inches. The Art Institute of Chicago and VAGA, New York. Friends of American Art Collection, image © 1996 The Art Institute of Chicago, 1930.934. All rights reserved. Photograph © 1996, The Art Institute of Chicago. All rights reserved.

C Minnie, Bethune Academy. *Baby Love.* Tagboard, oil pastels, marker, structure 22 by 14 inches, figure 5¾ by 10½ inches.

D Erin, Bethune Academy. *Back at Home.* Tagboard, oil pastels, marker, structure 22 by 14 inches, figure 4⅝ by 9¾ inches.

🖐 Try Your Hand
Making a Special Structure

Think of a structure that has special meaning to you.
1. Fold a large sheet of tagboard three ways.
2. Stand it up. Then make cutouts, such as windows and doors.
3. Draw and cut out a figure of yourself holding a symbol of strength.
4. Decorate the structure and the figure with water-based markers or crayons.
5. Stand them up by taping them to a sheet of construction paper.
What type of balance will your composition show?

Exploring Balance and Pattern **31**

Making a Print

Kenojuak Ashevak. *The Return of the Sun,* 1961. Stonecut, 24 by 36 inches. © West Baffin Eskimo Co-operative Ltd.

The pictures on these pages are called **relief prints.** They were made by transferring a design from one surface to another. Artists who make prints are called **printmakers.**

Printmakers prepare to make prints in many ways. First they draw a design on paper. Then they transfer the design to a flat surface called a **block,** or **plate.**

The printmakers of **A, B,** and **C** subtracted parts of their designs. The artist of **A** prepared her plate on a flat stone. She cut away the negative space of her design. The shapes of the sun, the animals, and the birds then became slightly raised. The printmaker of **C** carved away the negative space from a piece of wood. Point to the positive space in both **A** and **C.**

The plate can be made of materials such as a slab of clay, some cardboard, a meat tray, wood, stone, or linoleum. Some 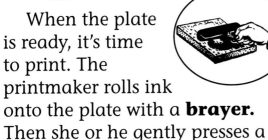 printmakers add to, or build up, their design on the plate. They use string, glue, paper shapes, and other materials. Other printmakers subtract, or carve away, parts of the design.

When the plate is ready, it's time to print. The printmaker rolls ink onto the plate with a **brayer.** Then she or he gently presses a paper on top of the plate. The last—and perhaps most exciting—step is to pull the print.

Printmakers usually go back to the plate to subtract or add something. They improve the design. Often they remove the ink from the plate and roll on another color. Then they print again on the same paper or on a new one.

Brian, Hoelscher Elementary. *Re-Leaf Tree*. Print plate, ink on paper, approximately 12 by 14 inches.

 Gerhard Marcks. *Bavarian Dance (Schuhplattler),* 1950. Woodcut on paper, 9½ by 4½ inches. Courtesy of Gerhard Marcks-Stiftung, Bremen, Germany.

Making a Print 33

Cultural Leaders

Prints of leaders in cultures become visual records of history. They offer clues about ideas, beliefs, and values of the culture. Which cultures are represented in the prints on these pages? To help you find out, read the credit lines of **A** and **B**. Point out objects and symbols in each print that tell more about the cultures and their leaders.

The student artist of **B** used two ways of printing. Here is how she made the rain dancer.

- She first brushed tea onto the center of a sheet of white paper.

- With crayons she then drew and colored the figure on a sheet of sandpaper.

- Next, she ironed the sandpaper design onto the dry, tea-stained paper.

Here is how she created the border designs.

- She made two printing stamps with slabs of clay.

- She pressed the inked stamp onto the border to make the print.

A

Max Weber. *Rabbi Reading*, 1919. Woodcut, printed in color, composition: 4³⁄₁₆ by 1¹⁵⁄₁₆ inches. The Museum of Modern Art, New York. Gift of Abby Aldrich Rockefeller. Photograph © 1996 The Museum of Modern Art, New York.

Sarah, Liestman Elementary. *Rain Dancer.* Sandpaper, crayon, ink, foam-board prints, 17¾ by 12 inches.

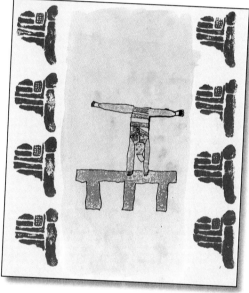

 Caitlin, Collins Intermediate. *Racer.* Sandpaper, crayon, clay stamp, ink, marker on paper, 12 by 14 inches.

 Erika, Collins Intermediate. *Olympic Star.* Sandpaper, crayon, clay stamp, ink, marker on paper, 12 by 14 inches.

Try Your Hand
Creating a Print of a Leader in Your Culture
1. Follow the instructions on page 34 for using sandpaper and crayons.
2. Turn to page 135 to learn how to make clay stamp prints.
3. Use two or three clay stamps and ink to make prints for the borders.

Where can you research your topic before you begin?

Which leader will you choose?

Which symbols will you include?

ARTIST AT WORK

Jaune Quick-to-See-Smith

(zhahn kwick-to-see-smith)

(1940–   )

Jaune Quick-to-See Smith. Photograph courtesy of Steinbaum Krauss Gallery, New York.

Jaune Quick-to-See-Smith did not have store-bought toys as a child. Instead she played in the woods and fields. She watched birds and animals in their natural homes. Her playthings were rocks, dirt, and ferns.

Today Quick-to-See-Smith is a well-known American Indian artist. But she still spends as much time as she can with nature. Sometimes she finds a bug or plant that she has never seen before. When this happens, she reads books that will teach her about the object. Quick-to-See-Smith also reads about history. She is very interested in the history of American Indians. As she reads, she gets ideas for her artworks.

Quick-to-See-Smith likes to help others learn about art. She helped raise money for a new arts building in Montana. Children who go to this center learn that art is important to everything they study. She has also helped artists form groups. In these groups, people learn from one another and share resources.

Quick-to-See-Smith sees herself as a teacher. She thinks of her artworks as her message. Many show scenes from nature. Others show her feelings about being an American Indian. She hopes that she can help people learn to think in new ways.

WRITE ABOUT ART

A Word About
Family Tree

This drawing celebrates the values and history of the artist's culture. She used visual symbols, such as horses, feathers, and trees, to show her family's history. Why might the horse be a most special symbol in this American Indian tradition?

Look at *Family Tree*. Imagine that this picture is on the cover of a book. What would the book be about? Where would the story take place?

Write Away

Think of a story that might go with Family Tree. Then draw a chart like the one shown. Complete the chart to show your story idea.

Story Title:

Setting:

Characters:

Chapter Titles
Chapter 1:
Chapter 2:
Chapter 3:

Story Summary:
This book is about

TALK ABOUT ART

Jaune Quick-to-See Smith. *Family Tree,* 1986. Pastel on paper, 30 by 22 inches. Collection of Bernice and Harold Steinbaum. Courtesy of Steinbaum Krauss Gallery, New York.

Look at A to answer these questions:

1. What do you see? Name the different kinds of lines you see. Discuss the artist's use of diagonal and horizontal lines. Find and name some color schemes.

2. How is *Family Tree* arranged? Explain how the composition is balanced. Discuss the artist's use of foreground, middle ground, and background. Discuss the artist's arrangement of triangles.

3. What does *Family Tree* mean? Would you say this is a fantasy drawing? Explain. Discuss what you think the visual symbols mean. How do you think the artist feels about her subject?

4. What's your opinion? What do you like best about the drawing? Does the artwork say anything about your own culture? Explain. Have your feelings about this drawing changed since you first saw it? Explain.

Wang Yani. *Little Monkeys and Mummy,* 1980. Ink and pigment on paper, 15 by 21 inches. © Wang Shiqiang. Courtesy of Byron Preiss Visual Publications, Inc./New China Pictures.

Compare A and B.

How are **A** and **B** similar and different? Point to the artwork with mostly neutral colors. How does each one tell a story about a family? What is the theme of these artworks?

A Word About
Little Monkeys and Mummy

This painting was created by an artist in China when she was only five years old. She spent a lot of time watching the monkeys. Then she painted them from memory. She has captured the lively movements of the monkeys. How do you think the artist feels about them?

Unit 2 **39**

PORTFOLIO PROJECT

Cultural Prints

Which animals are popular in your culture?
How can you show in a print how you feel about one of them?

1. Tape a clear plastic transparency to the table. Cut out a simple animal shape. Tape the back of it to the transparency's center.

2. Roll a color of ink over the transparency, or plate. Remove the animal shape.

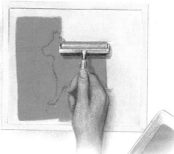

3. Draw in textures and some shapes of objects related to your animal theme.

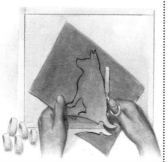

4. Gently press a sheet of paper over the plate. Pull the print. Let it dry.

5. With a paintbrush, paint the animal shape with two or three colors of ink. Paint shapes in the background, too. Add a border.

6. Press the same sheet of paper over the plate. Pull the print. Let it dry.

What colors did you use? Do they show a color scheme? Explain.
How did you show your theme?
Does the relief print show how you feel about the animal? Explain.

A

Brennan, Collins Intermediate. *Cardinal.* Ink print, tempera on paper, 8⅝ by 11¾ inches.

B

Katie, Collins Intermediate. *Fish of the Sea.* Ink print, tempera on paper, approximately 11 by 8½ inches.

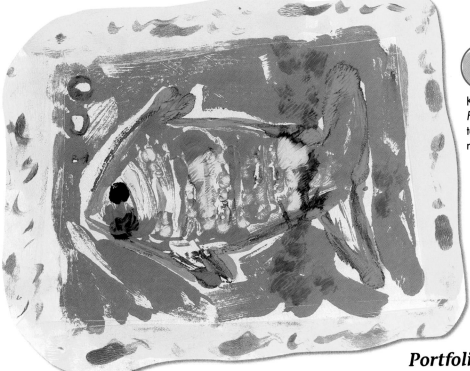

What Have You Learned?

Sketchbook Progress

1. What color schemes did you make?

2. Write the name of each hue in your color schemes.

3. Make a list of the secondary colors you made. What primary colors did you mix to make each one?

4. Make a list of the intermediate colors you made. What primary and secondary colors did you mix to make each one?

Portfolio Progress

Try Your Hand

5. Describe the colors you used in the first half of your work. Locate them on the color wheel. Which tints and shades did you make, as well?

6. What type of balance did you create in your stained-glass window? Describe the pattern or patterns in your artwork.

7. Write a paragraph that tells about your structure. Explain why it has special meaning for you. Describe the symbol you used to show strength.

8. For your print, did you choose a leader from the past or the present?

Portfolio Project

9. Which animal did you choose to represent your culture?

10. Describe why this animal is a good symbol.

11. What details did you use to show your feelings about this animal?

12. List the things you feel are successful about your print.

Unit Review

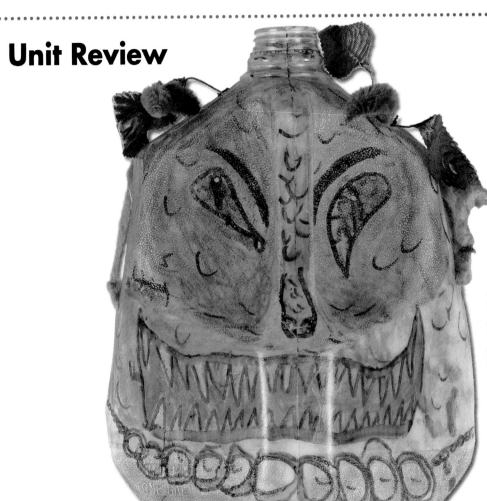

Johnson, Boone Elementary. *Milk-Jug Mask.* Plastic milk jug, markers, yarn, artificial leaves, 7½ by 10 inches.

1. What are the most important colors in this artwork? How does the artist make these colors important?

2. To what color group does each of these hues belong?

3. What mood does the color scheme create?

4. What type of balance does this artwork show? What other kinds of balance have you learned about?

5. What is a visual symbol?

6. What is a theme?

Art as a Cultural Record

Betye Saar. *Spirit Catcher,* 1976–1977. Mixed-media floor assemblage, 45 by 18 by 18 inches. Collection of the artist.

Art Can Say Many Things

Have you ever heard the expression "A picture is worth a thousand words"? What do you suppose it means?

Most artists might agree that artworks can say a lot. They usually require the viewer to think about, question, wonder about, or even disagree with the message.

In this unit, you'll learn about more artworks that say many things. They are three-dimensional artworks, or forms. You'll see sculpture as small as a necklace and as large as a building. You'll discover headgear and masks from faraway places. The artworks in this unit are real and abstract. They are imaginative and funny, serious and informative.

Which messages have you expressed through your art? Describe them to a friend. In doing so, you may find that a picture is worth a thousand words.

First Look

What do you think this artwork is about? Does it remind you of anything? Explain. How does it make you feel?

Masks and Headgear as Art

Perhaps you've made a mask. Masks are **three-dimensional** artworks. They have height, width, and depth. Together, these three dimensions create **form.**

Masks are forms that can say many things. When you wear them, they change the way you look and feel. The mask in **A** was worn by a king. He believed it would give him power. Suppose you could explore the tactile textures of **A**. How might the red tassel made from a parrot's feathers feel? Would the white shells feel hard or soft? smooth or rough? warm or cool? Describe the tactile texture of the leopard's fur that covers the face, the monkey's hair that forms the beard, and the grass behind the head.

Discuss the visual textures of **A**. Which objects look shiny? Which one appears dull?

Perhaps you've seen **B**, the mask of Tutankhamen (King Tut). It is more than 3,000 years old. In 1922 archeologists discovered King Tut's burial tomb. Included among the treasures they found was King Tut's mask. It was made of gold and a blue stone called lapis lazuli. Discuss the visual and tactile textures of King Tut's mask. Tell how you might feel if you wore it for a special event.

Artist unknown. *Tutankhamen, mask from mummy case,* ca. 1340 B.C. Gold, lapis lazuli, and carnelian, height 21¼ inches. Egyptian Museum, Cairo. Photograph © Boltin Picture Library.

Seeing, Planning, Thinking Like an Artist

Make a sketch of a mask your friend might wear.
First, interview your friend to find out ways that she or he would like to feel and look. Some examples might be an excited monster or a happy clown.
Next, ask your friend to comment on the sketch you've made.
Make more sketches based on the comments.
Finally, make a list of materials you might use to make the mask.

Artist unknown, Northwestern Plains Indian. *War Bonnet,* ca. 1885. Feathers, wooden rods, porcupine hair, wool, ermine, and felt, length 28 inches. Buffalo Bill Historical Center, Cody, Wyoming. Chandler-Pohrt Collection, Gift of Mr. and Mrs. Richard A. Pohrt.

Artist unknown, Tlingit (Chilkat). *Crest Hat.* Twined brim with painted killer whale, topped by carved raven. Catalog No. 221.177, Department of Anthropology, Smithsonian Institution.

Ceremonial Headdresses

People in many cultures wear hats designed to protect them from the weather. Artists design some hats to be **decorative,** as well as **functional.** These hats please the eye while they protect the head.

The feather bonnet in **A** was made of materials from the artist's environment. It was worn by an American Indian dancer during ceremonies. Name some visual and tactile textures in **A**.

The crest hat in **B** was worn by a member of another American Indian cultural group. Two artists, a weaver and a carver, worked together to make it. Point to the killer whale painted on the brim. Would you say the painting is abstract or realistic? How would you describe the textures of the raven carved on top?

How to
Make Paper Hats

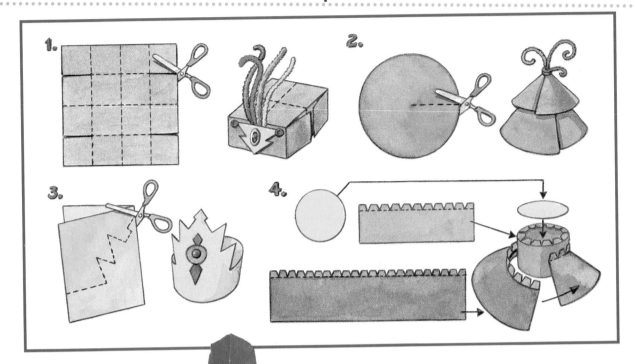

1.

2.

3.

4.

C

Nathan, Brentwood Elementary. *Band Hat.* Heavy paper, tempera, marker, feather, metallic pipe cleaner, 6½ by 8 by 10¾ inches.

Try Your Hand
Making a Special Hat

Make a decorative and functional hat to wear on a special occasion.

1. Make a sketch of the design for your hat.
2. Gather lightweight materials for decorations.
3. Study the instructions in How to Make Paper Hats above.
4. Choose a hat style. Have fun creating!

D

Ryan, Brentwood Elementary. *Double-decker Hat.* Heavy paper, tempera, marker, glitter glue, feathers, metallic pipe cleaners, diameter 11⅜, height 10¾ inches.

Masks and Headgear as Art **49**

Lesson 8

Expression Through Modern Art

The artworks on these pages suggest a sense of motion called visual **rhythm.** The elements of art appear to dance, swirl, reel, bend, twist, and spin. What lines do you see? Point to organic and geometric shapes. Which ones create patterns of motion?

These modern artworks are done in a **nonobjective** style. They do not suggest a scene or objects that anyone might recognize. Read the credit lines to find out what kinds of **media** the artists used to make them. Which sculpture is largest? Which two are small?

Many artworks have a **center of interest.** Some are more noticeable than others. For example, the artist of **D** wanted to place **emphasis** on the circular

Frank Stella. *Thruxton 3X,* 1982. Mixed media on etched aluminum, 75 by 85 by 15 inches. Courtesy of the Shidler Group, Honolulu. © 1997 Frank Stella/Artists Rights Society (ARS), New York.

part of her composition. Point to the center of interest in **D.**

Which other elements of art and principles of design do you notice on these pages? How does each artwork make you feel?

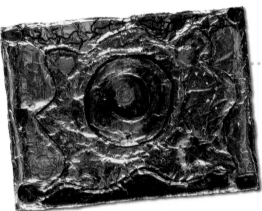

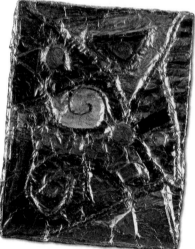

Naomi, Brentwood Elementary. *The Universe*. Cardboard, found objects, foil, markers, 11¼ by 8⅛ inches.

Anibal, Brentwood Elementary. *Floating Triangles*. Cardboard, found objects, foil, markers, 8½ by 11 inches.

Susan Stinsmuehlen. *Knight Giant, Oil and Wind*, 1985. Glass, metals, paint, wood, and mixed media, 27 by 32 inches. Private collection. Photograph courtesy of the artist.

Try Your Hand
Creating an Artwork that Shows Rhythm

1. Glue string, yarn, buttons, beads, and other found objects to a piece of cardboard. Show rhythm and pattern. Create a center of interest. Let the glue dry.
2. Sponge or brush a mixture of glue and water over a sheet of aluminum foil. Let it dry.
3. Gently press the aluminum foil onto the surface of the decorated cardboard. Fold it over the edges.
4. Use colored markers. Emphasize special lines and shapes by drawing on the aluminum foil.

A Claes Oldenburg. *Two Cheeseburgers, with Everything (Dual Hamburgers),* 1962. Burlap soaked in plaster, painted with enamel, 7 by 14¾ by 8⅝ inches. The Museum of Modern Art, New York. Philip Johnson Fund. Photograph © 1996 The Museum of Modern Art, New York.

Pop Art

The sculptures on these pages are inspired by food. They represent popular food items that are often mass-produced. Food, soup cans, soft-drink cans, telephones, typewriters, clothespins, and other common objects became subject matter for some artists during the 1950s. This style became known as **Pop Art** in Great Britain and North America. It poked fun at the many things people bought in stores.

Could the artist of **A** have squeezed anything else inside the two cheeseburgers? They appear brimming with gooey and lumpy parts. But they are hard as nails! Study the credit line to discover the **medium** the artist used. What mood do you think the artist intended to create?

B Donovan, Brentwood Elementary. *Pepperoni Pizza.* Ceramic, diameter 8¾, height 1¼ inches.

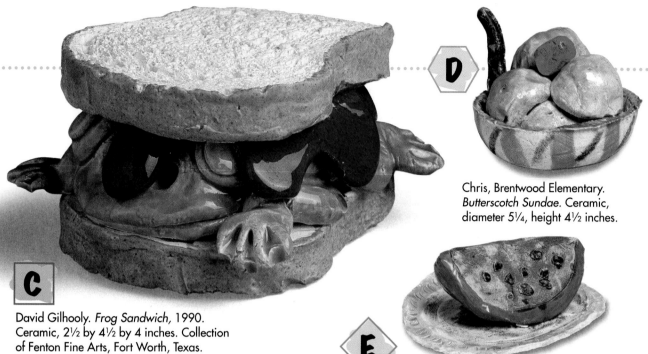

D

Chris, Brentwood Elementary. *Butterscotch Sundae.* Ceramic, diameter 5¼, height 4½ inches.

E

Amber, Brentwood Elementary. *Watermelon.* Ceramic, diameter 8⅝, height 3¼ inches.

C

David Gilhooly. *Frog Sandwich,* 1990. Ceramic, 2½ by 4½ by 4 inches. Collection of Fenton Fine Arts, Fort Worth, Texas. Photograph by David Wharton.

The artist of **C** made the **ceramic** artwork from **clay.** Clay is a soft, moist medium that is dug from the earth. First the artist shaped the clay and allowed it to dry. Then he baked it in a **kiln,** or a special oven. This process is called **firing** the clay because the kiln becomes as hot as fire. When the clay cooled, the artist painted it with **glaze.** Glaze is a mixture of water and minerals. Then he fired the sandwich sculpture again. This melted the glaze into the colorful glass surface that you see in **C**. How does **C** make you feel?

F

Ashley, Brentwood Elementary. *Chicken Taco.* Ceramic, diameter 6⅞, height 3 inches.

Try Your Hand
Making a Pop-Art Meal

As a class, create a Pop-Art meal of ceramic food items.

1. Sketch a design of a food item you'd like to bring to the meal.
2. Look on pages 136 and 137 for instructions about how to work with clay.
3. Make your sculpture with clay. Let it dry.
4. Paint it with acrylic paints or glazes.
5. Help your friends make a table setting. Present your dish for the Pop-Art meal.

Expression Through Modern Art

Say It with Architecture

Forms with curved edges

sphere

cone   cylinder

Forms with straight edges

pyramid   cube

slab

Moving of the Fairmount Hotel, San Antonio, Texas, March 30–April 4,1985.

Artists who design buildings are called **architects.** They make plans for schools, houses, stores, hotels, and other kinds of structures. Architects work with forms like those in **A.** Walls, closets, rooms, roofs, and elevators are examples of the forms they design. Like other forms, these have height, width, and depth.

Architects often combine forms in their designs. Point to and name some different forms you see in these pictures. Now imagine how each building would look with two or three additional forms.

Pictures **B** and **C** on these pages show hotels. One of the hotels is almost 100 years old. You can tell which one it is by looking closely. Notice the architectural style and building materials. This hotel, in **B**, was built in 1906. About 80 years later, it was moved and **renovated,** or renewed. The hotel weighed 3,200,000 pounds and stood 45 feet high. It was transported six blocks. This transfer is listed in the *Guinness Book of World Records* as the largest building move.

Westin-Bonaventure
Hotel, Los Angeles,
California.

C

D

The steps in planning a building begin
with gathering questions and answers.
What is the building for? Who will use it?
Where will it be? How much space is needed?
Next, the architect makes sketches of the **floor
plan** and then talks with the client again. Any
changes are marked on the sketches. Finally, the
architect makes a **blueprint,** or a copy of the
final drawing. Point to the blueprint on this page.

Seeing, Planning, Thinking Like an Artist

Use your imagination and drawing skills to draw a floor plan.
Include all rooms, hallways, closets, and doors that will be needed.
Make a pencil sketch first. Then redraw your final floor plan with a
blue marker.

Say It with Architecture   55

Louis Kahn, architect. The Kimbell Art Museum, Fort Worth, Texas.

Keepers of the Culture

Most communities have public buildings for special purposes. The art museum in **A** is open to the public for viewing artworks. This is where artwork is preserved for future generations.

Some art museums house international art collections. Others have paintings, drawings, and sculptures made by local artists. You can view some of these artworks in **galleries.** Galleries are large rooms inside the museum. In an art gallery you might see an art exhibition, or a display of artworks grouped according to a special theme. Tell about an art exhibition you have seen.

Perhaps you've met a **docent** in an art museum near you. A docent is a guide who shows you through art exhibitions in the museum. Docents have learned about the history of artworks and artists. Sometimes docents and other **museum educators** visit schools. They prepare students for a visit to the art museum. Would you like to have a **career** as a museum educator? Explain. What other careers might an art museum offer?

In some communities the art museum is part of an **art center,** or a cluster of fine-arts buildings. In addition to an art museum, an art center might have a theater for performing arts. It can also include a music building, a dance studio, and a fine-arts library.

How to

Make Some Forms for a Model

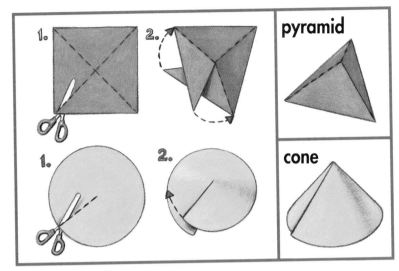

pyramid

cone

Katie, Natalie, and Stacy, Collins Intermediate. *Art Center Model.* Construction paper, colored craft paper, 14 by 12 by 5⅛ inches.

Keith, Scott, and Chris, Collins Intermediate. *Community Art Center.* Construction paper, colored craft paper, 14 by 12 by 5⅝ inches.

Architects plan and arrange the buildings in an art center. First they draw the blueprint. Then they make a **model,** or a miniature art center, to show the design. They often display the model on a table. Architects sometimes work with a **landscape architect.** This artist plans outdoor spaces—plants, fountains, walkways, and other items—around the buildings.

Try Your Hand

Making a Model of an Art Center

Work with friends to make a model of an art center.

1. In a small group, discuss ways buildings will be used and who will use them. You may want to create a blueprint of the art center.
2. Make buildings for the model. Create forms from construction paper or tagboard. Attach them together with a glue stick or tape. Use found objects for some forms.
3. Use markers for details such as windows and doors.
4. Arrange your model on a poster-board base. How can you add details to the outdoor spaces?

ARTIST AT WORK

Betye Saar

(beh-tee sahr)

(1926–)

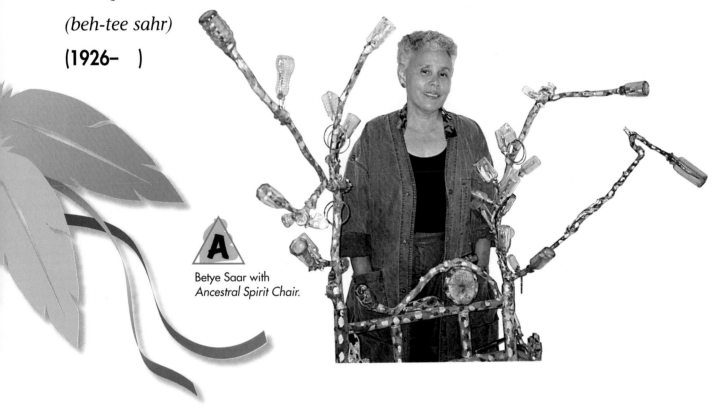

A Betye Saar with *Ancestral Spirit Chair.*

Betye Saar has collected things all her life. As a young girl in California, she liked to dig in her grandmother's backyard. She found pieces of glass, stones, and beads to collect. Saar sometimes used these items in gifts she made for others. She also used them in artworks she made with some of her family members.

As an adult, Saar became a designer. After a while, she began to make sculptures from the things she collected. The artist arranged some of the objects she collected in boxes for others to see. Sometimes her art showed her feelings about being African American. Sometimes her artworks were about her family.

Saar still makes art from things she finds. She uses objects from nature, such as shells, wood, bone, and leather. Saar likes to use materials that have belonged to others. She feels that these objects are special. They carry the memory of what they were into their new place in an artwork.

WRITE ABOUT ART

Look at *Spirit Catcher*. Betye Saar used many different materials to make this artwork.

List some of the materials the artist used. Then read your list. Suppose you could make something with these same materials. What would it be? Would it be a sculpture, something you could use, or both?

A Word About
Spirit Catcher

This artwork by an African American artist brings together objects from different cultures. It is modeled after a sculpture that holds special meaning to some people in China. Notice the bamboo, sticks, and string. Name some other found objects in the artwork.

Write Away

Write about the object you would make.

- Tell how you would put it together.
- Explain how you would use it.

Give your object a name.

TALK ABOUT ART

Look at A to answer these questions:

1. What do you see? Name at least five different objects in the sculpture. Point to anything you may have seen before. How would you describe the different textures? Point to positive and negative spaces.

2. How is *Spirit Catcher* arranged? Discuss how the artist connected the parts. What type of balance would you say the sculpture shows? Point to patterns of lines, shapes, and colors. Why do you suppose the artist chose a neutral color scheme?

3. What does *Spirit Catcher* mean? What does the Spirit Catcher remind you of? What do you think the artist was saying?

4. What's your opinion? If you saw this sculpture in a museum gallery, would you point it out to a friend? Why or why not? Would you like to make a sculpture with objects that are special to you? Why or why not? Have your feelings about this artwork changed since you first saw it? Explain.

Betye Saar, *Spirit Catcher*, 1976–1977. Mixed-media floor assemblage, 45 by 18 by 18 inches. Collection of the artist.

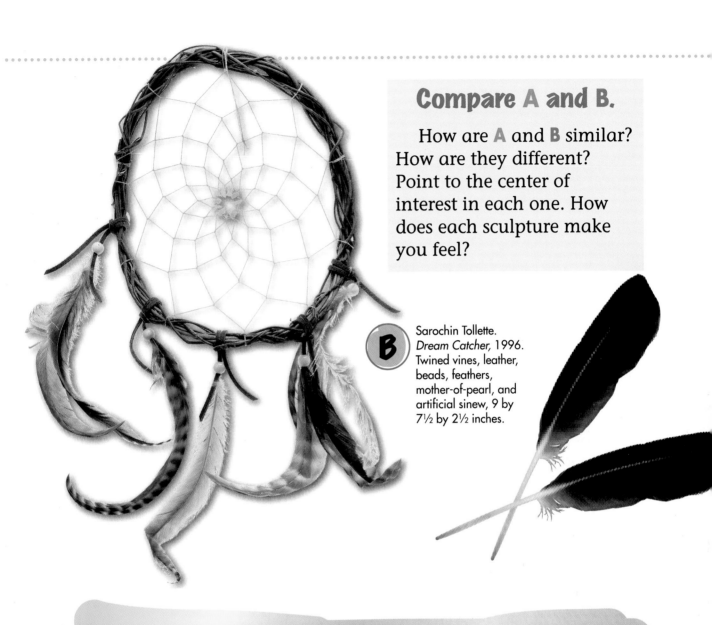

Compare A and B.

How are **A** and **B** similar? How are they different? Point to the center of interest in each one. How does each sculpture make you feel?

B Sarochin Tollette. *Dream Catcher,* 1996. Twined vines, leather, beads, feathers, mother-of-pearl, and artificial sinew, 9 by 7½ by 2½ inches.

A Word About

Dream Catcher

An artist made this dream catcher. The artwork honors special beliefs of the American Indian cultural group. This cultural group has many legends, or old stories passed down from old to young people. In one legend, the dream catcher is used to catch good dreams. Bad dreams pass through the hole in the center of the web.

PORTFOLIO PROJECT

Molding a Mini-Mask

You can make a miniature mask form to decorate your wall. Will your mini-mask look like a person? an animal? a character from a fantasy?

1. Shred newsprint and three analogous hues of tissue paper into thin strips. Put them into a blender that is half full of water. Your teacher will blend a thick pulp.

2. Scoop the pulp onto a piece of screen and blot it dry with paper towels.

3. Gently shift and press the pulp onto a small balloon form. Add layers of pulp to build up features from the surface. Let it dry.

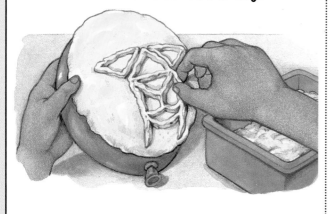

4. Remove the balloon. Punch holes in the edges of the mask form. Tie yarn, feathers, beads, and other decorative objects into the holes. Tie yarn across the back and display your mini-mask.

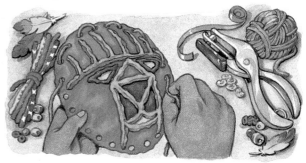

How does molding paper compare with molding clay?
What is successful about your mini-mask?
Where will you display your new artwork?

PORTFOLIO GALLERY

A

Mary Lee, Collins Intermediate.
Mini-Mask. Newsprint, tissue paper,
feathers, yarn, raffia, approximately
12½ by 12¾ by 2⅛ inches.

B

Chris, Collins Intermediate. *Mini-Mask.* Newsprint, tissue paper,
feathers, yarn, raffia, approximately 4¾ by 11½ by 1⅞ inches.

What Have You Learned?

Sketchbook Progress

1. What comments did your friend make about your sketch of a mask? How were your next sketches different from the first?

2. When you drew your floor plan, what sort of building were you planning? How does your blueprint meet the needs of people who will use the building?

Portfolio Progress

Try Your Hand

3. Which parts of your hat are functional? Which parts are decorative? On what special occasion could you wear this hat?

4. How would you describe the rhythm you created in your foil-covered artwork. Explain how you created a center of interest.

5. Describe how your food item is an example of Pop Art. Explain why you chose the food item you made for the Pop-Art meal.

6. Write a letter to the mayor about your model of an art center. Explain why your design should be chosen.

Portfolio Project

7. What subject did you choose for your mini-mask? Does this subject have special meaning for you? Explain.

8. What details did you add to your mask? Describe how adding details changed the feeling your mask expressed.

9. Is your mini-mask an example of realistic or abstract art?

10. Describe what you feel is successful about your project.

Unit Review

Sherlyn, Boone Elementary.
Cowgirl Artist. Clay, acrylic
paint, wood base, 6½ by 4¾
by 5⅝ inches, including base.

1. Write about the three dimensions of the artwork above.

2. Describe the subject.

3. Would you say this artwork is decorative or functional? Explain.

4. What medium did the artist use?

5. Is this artwork realistic or nonobjective? Explain your answer.

6. How is rhythm shown in artwork?

7. What is an art museum? What is a gallery?

8. Name three different careers of people who work in art museums. Describe each person's job.

Romare Bearden. *She-Ba,* 1970. Paper, cloth, and paint on board, 48 by 35⅞ inches. Wadsworth Atheneum, Hartford. The Ella Gallup Sumner and Mary Catlin Sumner Collection Fund. © Estate of Romare Bearden/ACA Galleries New York, Munich.

Art as Expression

Artists express their ideas, thoughts, and feelings by creating different types of artworks. Some artists explore art media, or the materials they use to create artworks. Other artists focus on a subject, or a topic, such as landscapes or animals. Still other artists express themselves through both the art medium and the subject.

The artworks in this unit show a variety of ways that artists express themselves. Some of these ways may appeal to you as career choices. For example, you'll learn about artists who cut out and arrange shapes and colors. You'll see compositions made with film. Then you might think about a career as a still-life photographer or as a filmmaker. You might enjoy viewing and making art about the land or the sea. Then you can consider a career in painting or earth art. Or you might be an artist who is interested in creating landscapes as a career. Then you'll probably take special notice of that subject and others like it.

First Look

What do you think is happening in this artwork?
What medium do you think the artist used?
What are your feelings when you look at this artwork?

Collage as Expression

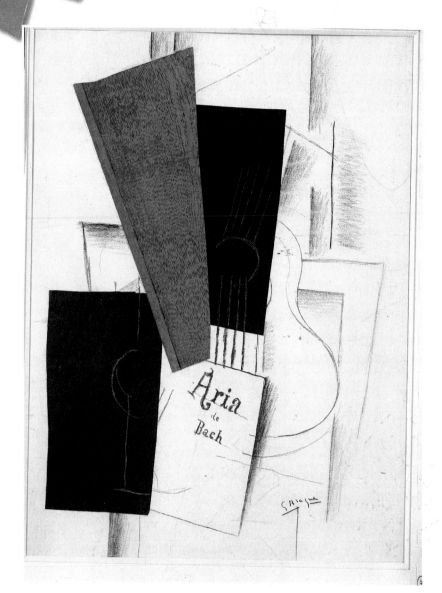

A Georges Braque. *Aria de Bach*, 1913. Collage with black paper, imitation wood, charcoal, and white chalk on paper, approximately 24½ by 18½ inches. National Gallery of Art, Washington. Collection of Mr. and Mrs. Paul Mellon. © 1997 Artists Rights Society (ARS), New York/ADAGP, Paris. Photograph by Dean Beasom.

A **collage** is made by arranging and gluing fabrics, paper, or found objects onto a surface. Collage artists often create visual stories by putting together objects that have certain meanings. What visual stories do you think the artists of **A**, **B**, and **C** might be telling? What hints can you find in the credit lines?

Each collage on these pages shows a **still life.** Artists use many different media to create still-life images. The artist usually arranges objects that can't move on their own. Examples are fruits, flowers, bottles, and musical instruments. This arrangement then becomes a model that the artist observes. The artist draws, paints, sculpts, or makes a collage. Which objects appear in the still-life collages in **A**, **B**, and **C**?

Pablo Picasso. *Still Life: Violin and Fruit,* 1913. Charcoal, colored papers, gouache, and painted paper, 25¼ by 19½ inches. Philadelphia Museum of Art: A. E. Gallatin Collection. © 1998 Estate of Pablo Picasso/Artists Rights Society (ARS), New York.

The artists of **A** and **B** created collages in an abstract style. Many shapes do not look realistic. Notice some examples of abstract shapes. How do you feel about abstract art? Would you like to explore this style in your own creations? Tell why or why not.

Marcus, Lackland Elementary. *The Golden Vase.* Tempera on paper, 12 by 18 inches.

Seeing, Planning, Thinking Like an Artist

Arrange several objects on your desk to serve as a model for a still life.
Cut images and shapes from magazine pages and construction paper.
Arrange and paste a still-life collage on a sheet of paper.
Will your collage be realistic or abstract?
Will you show neutrals or the colors of the rainbow?

Collage as Expression **69**

Henri Matisse. *The Thousand and One Nights,* 1950. Gouache on cut-and-pasted paper, 54¾ by 147¼ inches. Carnegie Museum of Art, Pittsburgh; Acquired through the generosity of the Sarah Mellon Scaife family, 71.23. © 1997 Succession H. Matisse, Paris/Artists Rights Society (ARS), New York. Photograph by Peter Harboldt, 1994.

Stories in Collage

Artists develop their own styles by studying the works of other artists, exploring their own ideas, and trying new ways of expression. Many artists are known for their individual styles. As you look at the collage above, you might ask, "What makes a Matisse a Matisse?" Studying the artist's style will help you know.

The French artist Henri Matisse enjoyed a long career as an artist. During that time he developed his own personal style. In about 1905 he joined with a small group of artists. The public made fun of these artists by calling them *Fauves.* This French word means "wild beasts." People then were not used to seeing the Fauve style. It included the use of pure, bright color.

Toward the end of his life, Matisse had become bedridden with health problems. He had even lost most of his eyesight. But he hadn't lost his love of pure, bright color. At about age 80, he used scissors to design large collages such as **A**. He cut abstract shapes from sheets of colored paper. "Cutting into living color

Illustration of symbols in A.

reminds me of the sculptor's direct carving," he said. Then he explained to his assistant exactly where to place the large shapes on the artwork.

The shapes in **A** tell about a fairy tale. Its title is written in the credit line. The drawings of visual symbols in **B** give more hints about the story. Notice the **variety** in the artwork. Point out the number of different symbols, colors, shapes, and lines. Matisse used variety to help show his style.

What's your opinion about this colorful collage? What mood does it create? How would you describe the movement in it? What is special about Matisse's style?

Try Your Hand
Making a Collage Mural

Work with a small group of artists.
1. Choose a story to tell with visual symbols.
2. Without drawing the shapes, cut and then arrange them on a large piece of butcher paper.
3. Paste down the shapes and add details. Hang your mural on the wall.
4. Ask each person in your group to tell a part of the story to the class.

Collage as Expression

Photography as Expression

About how many **still photographs** do you suppose you've seen in your lifetime? Hundreds? Thousands? Think about the many places where still photographs are displayed. **Photography,** as an art medium, is somewhat of a new way of making artworks.

The history of photography began fewer than 200 years ago. Other artists then were creating realistic drawings, paintings, and sculpture. But the new and extremely realistic photographs amazed people. Since then, **techniques,** or ways of making photographs, have improved. Today's photographers work with advanced equipment. Their cameras use a variety of lenses and high-speed color film.

Margaret Bourke-White. *Contour Plowing,* 1954. Black-and-white photograph. Margaret Bourke-White/LIFE Magazine. © Time, Inc.

Margaret Bourke-White taking photographs from the top of the Chrysler Building in New York. Courtesy of Margaret Bourke-White Estate. LIFE Magazine, © Time Warner, Inc.

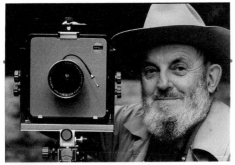

 Ansel Adams.

Ansel Adams. *Moon and Half Dome, Yosemite National Park,* ca. 1960. Black-and-white photograph. © 1995 by the Trustees of the Ansel Adams Publishing Rights Trust. All rights reserved.

Some modern photographers, such as those in **B** and **C**, prefer black-and-white to color film. Study their photographs in **A** and **D** to discover why. Notice the **shading,** or slight changes in the value of light or dark areas. Find dramatic shadows. See how curved and straight lines contrast against the areas next to them. Consider how vertical, horizontal, and diagonal lines stand out. All of these things affect the mood of each photograph.

Both **A** and **D** are **landscape** photographs. Landscapes show outdoor scenes such as rivers, lakes, valleys, mountains, and fields.

Seeing, Planning, Thinking Like an Artist

Use your sketchbook to draw a sketch of a landscape.
Write some notes.
Let your sketch become an idea to help you plan photographs you might take.

Photography as Expression 73

 Eadweard Muybridge. *Horse Galloping,* 1887. Collotype print. George Eastman House, Rochester, New York.

Moving Photography

How would you answer the question "Does a running horse have all four hooves off the ground at once?" In the 1870s, the photographer of **A** was hired to discover the answer to this question. The history of **motion pictures** on film began with his experiment.

The photographer lined up a series of still cameras beside a race track. Each camera had a string attached for the horse to trip as it ran past. Every few seconds a different camera clicked. Look again at **A**. What answer do you think the photographer discovered?

A second discovery came later. The photographer projected the still photographs in a rapid order, or quick motion. He found that the horse appeared to move. This **illusion** of motion caused the viewer to think the movement was real. It became the basis of **filmmaking.**

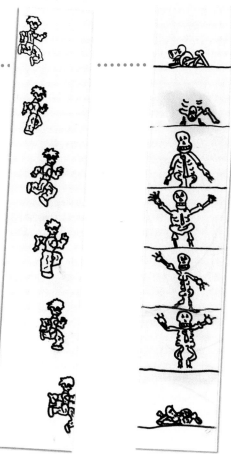

Many other discoveries have come from this experiment. For example, it led to the invention of the motion-picture camera. It changed the ways that other visual artists show animals in motion. It even sparked the beginnings of **animation.** Animation is the art of creating cartoonlike motion pictures for television and film. Would you like to have a career as an **animator**?

 B Richard, Allison Elementary. *Runner.* Filmstrip, 2 by 11 inches.

 C Rachel, Allison Elementary. *Mr. Bones.* Filmstrip, 2 by 11 inches.

Try Your Hand

Making an Animated Filmstrip

1. Think of an animal for your filmstrip. Draw some sketches of it moving in different ways.
2. On a strip of clear, heavy plastic, draw six frames of equal size.
3. With a thin-tipped marker, draw your animal in each frame. Show very slight changes in each frame.
4. Tape a sheet of paper to the glass plate of an overhead projector. Allow light to shine through an area about the width of one frame. Pull your cartoon strip quickly across the lighted area.

Does your strip show animation on the screen?

How could you make a longer strip?

Photography as Expression

Expressions About the Land

Robert Smithson.
Spiral Jetty, 1970.
Great Salt Lake, Utah.
Photograph ©
Gianfranco Gorgoni.

Artworks with landscape as the subject can be expressed in a variety of ways. The pictures on these pages show a type of expression called **site-specific** art. Each outdoor sculpture was designed for a special place. The place becomes a part of the sculpture. The sculpture helps define the place.

The **earthwork** in **A** is a jetty. It is a structure in water to protect the shoreline. Earthworks are sculptural forms made of soil, rocks, and sometimes plants. The materials for the earthwork in **A** came from the surrounding area. Which kinds of tools do you think were used to move soil into the spiral form? How does your eye travel around the sculpture? Find the center of interest.

Now try to imagine an 18-foot-high white nylon fence running through 24-1/2 miles of California countryside. The picture in **B** shows a part of just such an artwork. Hundreds of workers helped the artists construct this sculpture. During its fourteen days in existence, *Running Fence* made the wind visible. It caught the changing light as it stretched across gently rolling hills.

 Christo and Jeanne-Claude. *Running Fence, Sonoma and Marin Counties, California, 1972–1976.* Woven nylon fabric, stretched between steel poles, supported by steel cables, 18 feet by 24½ miles. © 1976 Christo. Photograph by Jeanne-Claude.

Unity is the way in which the elements of art and principles of design work together to create a feeling of harmony. How did the artists of both **A** and **B** use line to show unity? Would you like to have been a worker on one or both of these projects? Explain.

Seeing, Planning, Thinking Like an Artist

Plan a site-specific artwork for an area in or near your community. Decide on a theme.
Draw some sketches of your ideas.
Make a list of materials and workers needed to build the artwork.
Make a schedule to plan how long it will take to build the artwork.
What ideas or feelings will your artwork express?

Skyline of Dallas, Texas.

Wayne Thiebaud. *Apartment Hill,* 1980. Oil on linen, 65 by 48 inches. The Nelson-Atkins Museum of Art, Kansas City, Missouri (Purchase: acquired with the assistance of the Friends of Art).

Views of Land and Sea

You've seen that artists create landscapes in a variety of ways. Now look at the pictures on these pages. They show **cityscapes** and **seascapes.** Consider what you know about a landscape. Then define *cityscape* and *seascape.*

The photograph in **A** is a realistic record of a city at night.

How is it different from the painting of urban apartments in **B**? How did the artist of **B** emphasize the location of the apartments? What clues tell you that the subject is a cityscape? How does the painting make you feel? Would you like to live in this place? Tell why or why not.

Emmanuel, Allison Elementary. *Land and Sea.* Chalk pastels on paper, 18 by 12 inches.

Claude Monet. *Rocks at Port-Goulphar,* 1886. Oil on canvas, 32 by 25½ inches. Cincinnati Art Museum, Fanny Bryce Lehmer Endowment and The Edwin and Virginia Irwin Memorial 1985.282.

How do **C** and **D** make you feel? The artist of **D** was painting 100 years ago. He was part of a group of artists in Paris. They became known as **Impressionists** because they painted their impressions of what they saw. They recorded moments of everyday life as they saw and felt them. Impressionists usually painted outdoors. They wanted to show how the changing light made their subjects appear. Discuss light and shadows in the foreground, middle ground, and background of **D**. Imagine how this place would look at different times of day.

Try Your Hand

Drawing a Cityscape or a Seascape

1. Use chalk pastels to draw a cityscape or a seascape.
2. Think about the mood you want to create and how to show it.
3. Carefully spray your finished drawing with a clear fixative.
4. Display your drawing.

Expressions About the Land

TALK ABOUT ART

Romare Bearden. *She-Ba,* 1970. Paper, cloth, and paint on board, 48 by 35⅞ inches. Wadsworth Atheneum, Hartford. The Ella Gallup Sumner and Mary Catlin Sumner Collection Fund. © Estate of Romare Bearden/ACA Galleries New York, Munich.

Look at A to answer these questions:

1. What do you see? Find light shapes and then dark ones. Name at least six kinds of lines you see. Do the shapes appear flat or rounded? Explain. Describe the figures in the collage.

2. How is *She-Ba* arranged? What type of balance does the collage show? Why do you think the artist placed the smaller figure behind the queen?

3. What does the collage mean? To whom do you think the queen is waving? How would the meaning change if she were in a car? How can you tell that the queen is powerful? What do you think the artist was saying about the queen?

4. What's your opinion? Where might you display this collage? Why? Have your feelings about this collage changed since you first saw it? Explain.

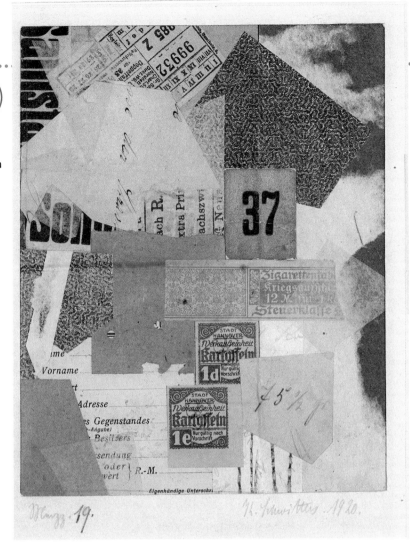

B

Kurt Schwitters. *Merz 19*, 1920. Collage, paper, 8 by 6¾ inches. Yale University Art Gallery. Gift of Collection Société Anonyme. © 1997 Artists Rights Society (ARS), New York/VG Bild-Kunst, Bonn.

Compare A and B.

How are the color schemes of **A** and **B** different? Discuss ways in which each artist showed unity and variety. What other similarities and differences can you point out?

A Word About

Merz 19

German artist Kurt Schwitters made this collage after World War I. *Merz* is a German slang word meaning "commercial." At that time, Schwitters felt that "everything [had] broken down and new things [would] have to be made out of the fragments." He put together the series of *Merz* collages from items others threw away. How does the artist's use of overlapping shapes add to the appeal of the design?

PORTFOLIO PROJECT

Making a Picture Collage

How would you and your friends look performing on a stage?
Would you play an instrument? read a poem? be an actor?

1. Cut and glue shapes of construction paper, wrapping paper, and wallpaper to show a place where people perform. It might be a stage, a city street, or an outdoor theater.

2. Photocopy a picture of your face and pictures of your friends' faces. Cut them out. Then cut out shapes of musical instruments, theater props, and clothing from extra paper. You might find some photographs in magazines, too.

3. Glue shapes together to make the shapes of the performers. Add body parts that show movement.

4. Glue the shapes of the performers, instruments, and props to the background. Add details with crayons or markers.

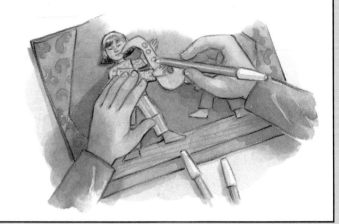

How did you show yourself, your friends, and the arts?
Does one figure stand out in your collage? Explain.
Describe how your composition shows unity and variety.

Lauren, Brentwood Elementary. *The Trumpeter.* Collage on paper, 15 by 13 inches.

 Carmen, Brentwood Elementary. *Opera Star.* Collage on paper, 16 by 13 inches.

What Have You Learned?

Sketchbook Progress

1. Describe your still life. Is it realistic or abstract? Which colors did you use?

2. What place did you sketch in your landscape? What notes did you write?

3. What place in your community did you decide to sketch for your site-specific art plan? Why did you choose this place? How will your site-specific artwork fill the needs of the people who use this area?

Portfolio Progress

Try Your Hand

4. What story did you and your group express in your group mural? How do the colors and shapes you used help to tell the story?

5. As you pulled your filmstrip across the overhead-projector plate, did the animal you drew appear to be moving?

6. Did you draw a cityscape or a seascape? Why did you make the choice you made? Do you have special feelings about cities or the ocean? Explain.

Portfolio Project

7. Did you use a variety of colors and shapes in your collage? Describe the color scheme you used. How does your choice of colors and shapes add to the ideas you wanted to express?

8. What details did you add to your collage with markers or crayons?

9. Did you show movement in your collage? How?

10. Give your finished artwork a title.

Unit Review

Steve, Smith Elementary. *Untitled.* Cardboard, tagboard, cotton, and crayon collage, 14 by 18 inches.

1. Describe the medium and subject of the artwork shown on this page.

2. Is this student artwork abstract or realistic? Explain.

3. Discuss the colors and the neutrals.

4. Describe the unity, variety, and patterns.

5. Is the artwork on this page a cityscape? Explain.

6. How are a landscape and an earthwork similar? How are they different?

7. Who were the Impressionists? What did they want to show in their work?

8. Describe the work of Romare Bearden.

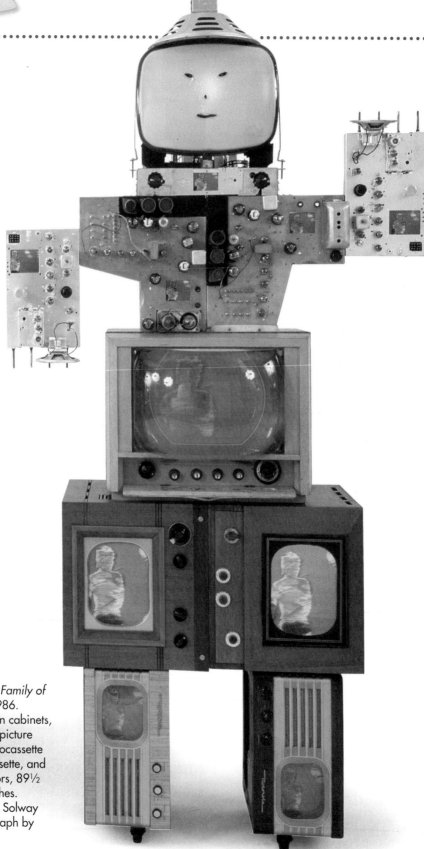

Nam June Paik. *Family of
Robot: Uncle*, 1986.
Vintage television cabinets,
vintage chassis, picture
tube, paint, videocassette
player, videocassette, and
television monitors, 89½
by 45 by 25 inches.
Courtesy of Carl Solway
Gallery. Photograph by
Cal Kowal.

Traditions and Changes in Art

Who would have dreamed long ago that electricity and gases could make beautiful colors in glass? Weavers from centuries past could not have imagined using a computer to design their blankets.

The passing of time often brings with it change. Cultures take on new ways of doing things. Fashion design, such as clothing and hairstyles, changes from year to year. Body styles for cars and trucks change with time. Changes come about for types of telephones, toasters, and televisions.

This unit tells about ways that some things change and others stay the same. You'll read about rapidly changing fields of art and areas of art that still rely on traditional guidelines. As you read, ask yourself why some things change and others stay the same.

First Look

What do you see in the picture? Point to parts of it that are old. What kind of mood do you think the artist wanted to show?

Old Traditions, New Ways

You've seen how artists use glass to make stained-glass windows. Glass is also a good medium for decorative parts of jewelry. This medium dates back at least 4,000 years. It has been a material for containers of all shapes and sizes. More recently, artists have made glass objects filled with neon and other rare gases. When mixed with electric power, these gases become colorful.

Point to the neon sign in **A**. During the early 1900s, this glass artwork became a familiar symbol. It stood for a brand of children's shoes. Notice how the lines of the neon glass emphasize shapes behind them.

 Artist unknown. *Neon Sign for Buster Brown Shoes,* ca. 1930. The American Advertising Museum, Portland, Oregon.

 Paul Seide. *Frosted Radio Light* from the *Spiral Series,* 1987. Blown glass, manipulated and charged with neon and mercury vapor from a transmitted radio field, 19⅓ by 21½ inches. The Corning Museum of Glass. Part gift of Mike Belkin.

Lauren, Raul B. Fernandez Elementary. *Swirly Curls*. Tempera on paper, 12 by 18 inches.

Rene, Raul B. Fernandez Elementary. *Untitled*. Tempera on paper, 18 by 12 inches.

With your finger, draw around the lines of the glass sculpture in **B**. The lines create spiral paths. See how the spirals lead your eye to create a feeling of visual rhythm. Point to other spiral lines on these pages. The artist of **B** liked the Fauve style of using colors. How is this artwork similar to Fauve painting?

Seeing, Planning, Thinking Like an Artist

Suppose that you choose sculpting glass as a career. How might your glass sculpture designs be similar to and different from the designs on these pages?
Practice drawing different kinds of lines, such as spirals.
Use markers to make shapes of bright colors.
Then imagine how you might work the lines, shapes, and colors into a glass sign or sculpture.
Make some sketches of your plans.

Old Traditions, New Ways   91

Navajo woman weaving on a vertical loom.

A

B

Artist unknown, American Indian, Southwest Navajo. *Blanket,* 19th century. Double-faced weave, 76¼ by 52½ inches. Cincinnati Art Museum, Gift of Mrs. C. Gordon Neff. 1937.373.

Weavings and Computers

In the Navajo tradition, women have woven beautiful and useful blankets for hundreds of years. Picture **A** shows a Navajo woman weaving on a **loom** in modern times. The **eye-dazzler blanket** in **B** is about 100 years old. It is an example of a type of **weaving** that shows colorful diamond shapes. This blanket has different designs on the back and front sides. Notice how bright colors are contrasted with each other. How do the black and white lines help emphasize the diamond shapes?

How would you describe the color schemes in **B**? What type of balance do you see? How did the artist show rhythm? Discuss unity and variety as principles of design in the blanket.

92   *Lesson 13*

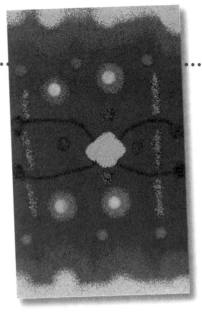

 Weaver refers to her computer as she weaves the design on her loom.

Now look at the weaver in **C**. Her tools are both similar to and different from the tools of the Navajo weaver. Notice the computer screen in **C**. The weaver has created a design on the computer. She is weaving the same design on a loom.

 Amanda, Oakwood Terrace Elementary. *Blanket Design*. Computer-generated blanket design, 11 by 8½ inches.

 Felipe, Hogg Elementary. *Striped Weaving*. Woven yarn, approximately 12 by 16 inches.

Try Your Hand
Creating Your Own Weaving
1. Study the guidelines on pages 138 and 139 to help you weave.
2. Choose colors of yarn that will show contrast.
3. Plan other ways to give your weaving unity and variety.
4. Weave your design on a loom.
5. Add details, such as beads, feathers, and sticks.

Careers That Keep Up with the Times

Do you have a favorite comic strip? Comic strips are types of **cartoons,** which are meant to make you laugh. The drawing in **A** is a cartoon. The artist is poking fun at the many ways that people judge artworks.

The artist in **C** drew the **editorial cartoon** in **D**. As an **editorial cartoonist,** his goal is to involve the reader in what is happening in the news. He has received many awards, and he is self-taught. "I used to come home from school and just draw," he explained. Today his editorial cartoons appear daily or weekly in newspapers nationwide.

"He knows all about art, but he doesn't know what he likes."

 James Thurber. *"He knows all about art, but he doesn't know what he likes,"* 1943. © 1943 James Thurber. © 1971 Rosemary A. Thurber. From *Men, Women & Dogs,* published by Harcourt Brace.

Mary, Eanes Elementary. *Editorial Cartoon.* Marker on paper, 11 by 8½ inches.

C Ben Sargent.

D Ben Sargent. *Heartless. Brainless. Cowardly. All of the Above.*, April 30, 1995. Editorial cartoon for the *Austin American-Statesman.* Courtesy of the artist.

Would you like a career as an editorial cartoonist? Here are some guidelines:

- Use **exaggeration.** Emphasize something or someone. Make the proportions appear unusual.

- Draw some **symbols.** Think of signs or objects that stand for something else.

- Apply **labels.** Write some words or phrases to identify people or causes.

- Create **caricature.** Draw a person's face in such a way that it is changed but you can still tell who it is.

Find examples of these guidelines in the cartoon in **D.**

Seeing, Planning, Thinking Like an Artist

Make some sketches of cartoons you might create. Maybe you'll experiment with creating a comic strip. Or think of something in the news that you'd like to poke fun at.

Show some friends your cartoon sketches.

Do they see the humor in your cartoon?

 A Sindelfingen. *Mercedes-Benz Type 500 K Special Roadster,* 1936. The National Automobile Museum, Reno, Nevada.

Industrial Designers

Somewhere between the time an idea is born and the time an item lands on store shelves, an **industrial designer** makes some decisions. This artist decides how items will look, feel, and function. Henry Dreyfuss, who designed for industry, explained, "What we work on is going to be ridden in, sat upon, looked at, talked into, activated, operated, or in some way used by people . . . ."

During the 20th century, industrial artists have created designs for things like cars, telephones, vacuum cleaners, sewing machines, and jet airplanes. Their designs combine comfort, function, beauty, and safety in products.

Look at the 1936 Special Roadster in **A**. What type of artist do you think designed it? Does it look comfortable? functional? beautiful? Why are safety standards of today different from the ones in 1936?

Natalie, Eanes Elementary. *Musical Car.* Marker on paper, 12 by 9 inches.

Jessica, Cambridge Elementary. *Automotive Man.* Marker on paper, 12 by 18 inches.

Should you choose industrial design as a career, you might work on things as simple as a paper clip. Or they might be just as complicated as a computer. You'd always be learning what's new and then you'd be improving upon that. You'd ask yourself questions like these: *What purpose will the object I am designing have? How can I make it affordable, functional, and attractive?*

✋ Try Your Hand

Designing a Cartoon Character's Car

1. Think of a new design for a car that your favorite cartoon character might like to drive.
2. Use tempera paints or markers to show your cartoon character with the new car.

How can your imagination help you create the design?

Will the car be comfortable, functional, beautiful, and safe?

The Tradition of Making Portraits

 A

Kano Tan'yu. (Detail) *Sakuma Shogen,* Edo period, ca. 1636. Ink and color on silk, 25⅛ by 11⅛ inches. © Shinju-an Temple, Kyoto, Japan. Photograph courtesy of Kyoto National Museum.

 B

Paula Modersohn-Becker. *Old Peasant Woman,* 1905. Oil on canvas, 30¼ by 23⅛ inches. The Detroit Institute of Arts, Gift of Robert H. Tannahill. Photograph © 1996 The Detroit Institute of Arts.

Portraits are artworks that show likenesses of real people or animals. How do you think the people in these portraits feel? Read the credit lines. Find out which ones were painted in the 17th century. Which ones were painted in the 20th century? What is similar about these portraits? What is different?

Portrait artists often make sketches of people in different **poses,** or positions. Sometimes they sketch them in natural positions. A person who poses for an artist is called a **model.** Read the credit line to find out the name of the model in **C.** Who was the artist? This artist created a portrait of himself, or a self-portrait.

Rembrandt van Rijn. *Self-Portrait,* 1659. Oil on canvas, 33¼ by 26 inches. Andrew W. Mellon Collection. © 1996 Board of Trustees, National Gallery of Art, Washington, D. C. Photograph by Richard Carafelli.

D

Elizabeth Catlett. *Two Generations,* 1979. Lithograph, 22 by 29 inches. © 1998 Elizabeth Catlett/Licensed by VAGA, New York, NY.

Seeing, Planning, Thinking Like an Artist

Make some sketches of a friend.
Practice showing her or him in different poses.
How does each pose change the way you feel about the portrait?

Clanra Maria Nauen-von Malachowski. *Little Girl in a Blue Apron*, ca. 1938. Oil on board, 27 by 19 inches. Städtisches Museum, Monchengladbach. © 1997 Artists Rights Society (ARS), New York/VG Bild-Kunst, Bonn. Photograph by Wolfgang von Contzen.

Creating a Portrait

Before cameras were invented, artists made portraits with brushes and other tools. They made portraits of friends and relatives. Some artists had careers making portraits of queens, kings, and other wealthy people. Why do you think some people today still choose to have their portraits drawn, painted, or sculpted?

The portrait in **A** was painted about 75 years ago. Does it look as though it might have been painted today, as well? What is unusual about the position of the model's head? Why do you suppose the artist painted it that way? What do the clothing and chair tell you about the model? What is the mood of this portrait?

Proportions of the face show how facial features relate to each other. Use your finger to measure proportions in **A**. The eyes are about halfway between the top of the head and the bottom of the chin. What do the model's eyes tell you about her? Which other proportions can you measure?

How to
Draw a Person's Face

1. Fold a sheet of paper once vertically.

2. Fold the same paper horizontally once, then twice.

3. Follow your guidelines to draw a shape for a head. It can be an oval, a square, a circle, or another shape. Then draw the neck, hair, and ears.

4. Draw facial features. The eyes are about halfway down. The nose is above the bottom guideline and the mouth is below.

Try Your Hand
Creating a Portrait

1. Find a model for your portrait. Ask the model to pose for you.
2. Make some sketches of your model's face. Use the guidelines above to help you.
3. On a larger sheet of paper, create a portrait of your model. Use crayons, oil pastels, chalk pastels, tempera paint, or another medium.
4. Add background details to help the viewer understand your model.

What pose will you show?

The Tradition of Making Portraits

Nam June Paik

(nam joon pahk)

(1932–)

Nam June Paik in his installation *Fish Flies on Sky*, 1976. Photograph by Peter Moore, © 1998 Estate of Peter Moore/Licensed by VAGA, New York, NY.

Can a television set be a type of art? Nam June Paik believes that it can. For more than 30 years, he has been making art from TVs, video pictures, and music.

The artist was born in North Korea, where he took piano lessons as a child. In 1949, his family left Korea for Hong Kong. Then they moved to Japan. There the young man studied art history and continued his study of music. Later, while living in Germany, he explored using recorded sounds in his music.

TV soon caught his interest. He bought 13 used TVs. Then he put them together with three pianos and noisemakers for an art show. He tried many ways of changing video pictures on a TV screen. At about the same time, he built his first robot. He used old TVs and radios as parts for the robot.

Nam June Paik says that he wants those who see his artwork to be entertained. He also wants them to find meaning in it. His assemblages have been exhibited all over the world. His artwork shows a new way to look at TV.

WRITE ABOUT ART

Look at *Family of Robot: Aunt and Uncle*. These robots are more than 7 feet tall! Do they seem friendly or unfriendly?

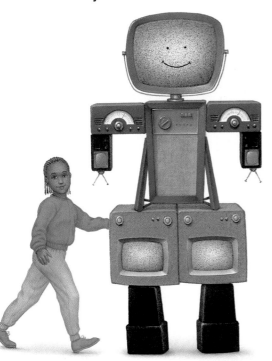

Write Away

Suppose these robots belonged to you. Write a story about you and the robots. Before you begin, think about the kind of story you will write. Will your story be funny? Will it tell about an adventure? a mystery? Then think about the robots. Do these robots look for mischief? Or do these robots try to avoid mischief?

As you write your story, remember to
• tell where the story takes place.
• give your story a beginning, a middle, and an end.
• think of a title for the story.

A Word About
Family of Robot: Aunt (left) and Uncle (right)

These robots are **assemblages,** or sculptures made by joining objects or parts of objects together. Altogether, *Family of Robot* includes grandparents, parents, aunts, uncles, and children. They represent generations and change. Each piece is an assemblage of old radio cabinets and TV sets. However, Nam June Paik replaced the old electronic hardware with new parts. The TVs show images from many sources.

TALK ABOUT ART

Nam June Paik. *Family of Robot: Aunt* and *Uncle,* 1986. Vintage television cabinets, vintage chassis, picture tube, paint, videocassette player, videocassette, and television monitors, each approximately 89½ by 45 by 25 inches. Courtesy of Carl Solway Gallery. Photograph by Cal Kowal.

Look at A to answer these questions:

1. What do you see? Describe the various parts of each robot. Name the shapes and forms you see. Discuss the various textures on the robots.

2. How is the assemblage arranged? How does the design show that the same artist created both assemblages? Describe the artist's use of both unity and variety. If you could hear the robots, how might each one sound? Compare the faces and arms of each robot. How are they different? How would you describe the proportions of the different parts of each robot?

3. What does *Family of Robot* mean? Are these realistic or fantasy sculptures? Suppose the artist hadn't installed new electrical parts to show modern moving images. Would the meaning of the assemblage have changed? Explain. Tell how the artist introduced humor into his sculptures. What do you think the artist intended to say?

4. What's your opinion? Why do some artists create sculptures with recycled objects? If you could ask this sculptor a question about his artworks, what would it be? Have your feelings about *Family of Robot* changed since you first saw the robots? Explain.

Compare **A** and **B**.

How are the materials in **A** and **B** similar? different? Compare the proportions of the head to the rest of the body in **A** and **B**. Each robot in **A** is about the size of a telephone booth, while **B** is not quite 2 feet tall. Does the size of each artwork help you understand what each artist was saying? Explain. Where would you display each artwork?

A Word About

Hemis Kachina

This kachina doll was carved by an artist from the Hopi cultural group. The doll's purpose was to teach Hopi children about ideas, beliefs, and values of their culture. Simple, wooden kachina dolls were given to children as their first toys. Some American Indian artists today still make kachina dolls.

Artist unknown, Hopi. *Kachina Figure*, ca. 1920s. Wood and feather, 22¾ by 8½ inches. © Denver Art Museum, Hopi Kachina #1927.27.

PORTFOLIO PROJECT

Creating an Assemblage

How can your imagination help you recycle found objects to create an assemblage? Think of an original industrial design. Will it be a robot that does chores for you? a new type of car? a bicycle for space travel?

1. Collect some found objects. Arrange them in different ways. Imagine an industrial design.

2. Ask a friend to help you put the forms together. Use masking tape, a stapler, paste, string, or wire. Maybe your teacher can use a glue gun to help, too.

3. Paint the assemblage once with gesso, then with tempera paints.

4. Attach as many details as you like. Use pipe cleaners, buttons, yarn, tissue paper, and other objects.

What is the purpose of your design? What makes it special?
Imagine having a working object made from your design.
What would you call it?

PORTFOLIO GALLERY

Gail, Tom, Brittany, John, Andy, and Adrianne, Eanes Elementary. *Future Car.* Found objects, gesso, acrylic paint, 8⅜ by 19⅝ by 7 inches.

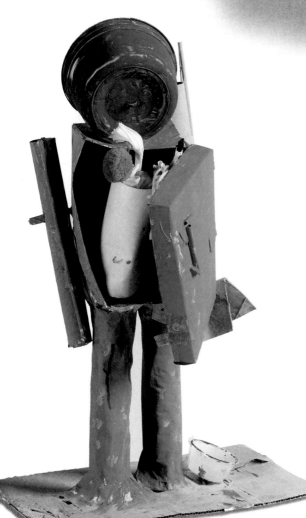

Matt, Laura, Hunter, Margo, Robert, Kathleen, Vinnie, and Margo, Eanes Elementary. *Robot.* Found objects, gesso, tempera paint, approximately 15⅞ by 9¾ by 26⅜ inches, including base.

What Have You Learned?

Sketchbook Progress

1. How did you use lines, colors, and shapes in your glass-sculpture plan?

2. What idea did you express in your cartoon? How did you make this idea humorous?

3. Which sketch best expresses your feelings about your friend? Explain.

Portfolio Progress

Try Your Hand

4. Do the colors of yarn in your weaving show contrast? Explain. How did you give your weaving unity and variety?

5. Have you ever seen a car like the one you designed? What would your friends say if they saw a car made from your design?

6. What details did you add to help the viewer know about your portrait model? What would be a good title for this portrait? Explain.

Portfolio Project

7. How did you decide which found objects to use? Do the objects have anything in common?

8. Do the colors and details you chose have a special meaning? Do they serve a particular purpose?

9. If your assemblage were a machine, what would its purpose be?

10. Did this activity cause you to see some common objects in a new way? Explain.

Unit Review

Luis, Campbell Elementary. *Woven Hanging.* Woven yarn, bamboo rod, 15⅝ by 20½ inches.

1. How did the artist create the artwork above?

2. What materials did the artist use?

3. Describe the colors. Where did the artist show contrast?

4. List the guidelines for creating an editorial cartoon.

5. List classroom objects designed by industrial designers.

6. Draw the guidelines for creating a portrait of a face.

David Bates. *The Whittler,* 1983. Oil on canvas, 96 by 78 inches. Archer M. Huntington Art Gallery, The University of Texas at Austin, Michener Collection Acquisition Fund, 1983. © David Bates. Photograph by George Holmes.

Many Kinds of Art and Artists

In this book, you've seen many kinds of artworks from around the world. You've read about people who've chosen art as their career. And yet, even an entire library couldn't show all of the artworks and artists in the world.

As an artist, you know that your artworks are original—unlike those of anyone else. You may be developing your own style of making art. You probably have at least one or two favorite media to use. With that in mind, think about all of the artists in the world. How many different styles must they have created? Could you even count the numbers of ways they have used media?

As you read, consider all that you have learned about art and artists. Ask yourself, *How can I learn more about the lives of the artists? Which people, places, and events in history might have influenced the artists?* Look back at other images in the book. Then ask yourself, *What have I learned? How can I apply this information to my own artworks?*

First Look

What type of artist is in the painting?
What else do you see?
How does the painting make you feel?

Stories and Symbols

Faith Ringgold. *Church Picnic Story Quilt,* 1988. Tie-dyed, printed fabrics, acrylic on cotton canvas, 76 by 76 inches. Collection of the High Museum, Atlanta, Georgia. Gift of Don and Jill Childress through the 20th Century Art Acquisition Fund. © 1988 Faith Ringgold. Photograph by Gamma I.

You have seen many artworks about cultural heritage. The wall hangings on these pages tell you stories about the artists' cultures. They show important events or objects with meaning.

The artists of **A** and **B** used **mixed media,** or a mixture of two or more media. Look closely to find both paint and **fabric,** or woven cloth. Notice the types of geometric shapes made of fabric. These **quilt blocks** form the borders of **A** and **B**.

Look closely at **A**. Artist Faith Ringgold wrote a story on the top and bottom borders. It tells about an event in her childhood. Why do you think she calls this artwork a **story quilt**?

In the center is a larger **canvas.** It is a closely woven cloth on which the artist painted. The painting shows what's happening in the story. Which clues tell you something about the event? What is the story quilt about?

Miriam Schapiro. *Wonderland*, 1983. Fabric and acrylic on canvas, 90 by 144 inches. © Miriam Schapiro. Courtesy of Steinbaum Krauss Gallery, New York.

Artist Miriam Schapiro calls her artwork in **B** a **femmage.** It is a type of collage that includes traditional fabric art made by women. Schapiro intends to pay honor to the beauty and usefulness of **needlework.** Examples of needlework are embroidery and quilting.

Notice the large, stitched sign at the center of **B**. How does it explain the **theme,** or message, of the femmage? Let your eye travel to aprons and other examples of needlework. How would you describe the balance?

How does the artist's use of patterns create visual rhythms? Find examples of at least eight objects that you might see in a kitchen. Why do you suppose Schapiro included them in her femmage?

Discuss ways that both **A** and **B** show unity and variety. How are **A** and **B** similar? Name ways in which they're different. Have your feelings about either of these artworks changed since you first saw them? Explain. If you could hang them on a wall, which place would you choose?

Stories and Symbols 113

Pictographs and Portraits in History

American Indian cultural groups of long ago used sign language and the spoken word to communicate. They also drew and painted **pictographs,** or pictures, on cave walls and animal hides. Pictographs helped them record the ideas, beliefs, and values of their culture. Like story quilts and femmages, pictographs tell visual stories. They record the history of certain cultural groups.

 Pictograph, Seminole Canyon State Historical Park, Texas.

The pictographs in **A** were painted on a canyon wall hundreds of years ago. The artist used natural dyes from nearby soils and plants. The figures you see may be religious leaders who were known as healers. What other information can you discover by studying the pictographs in **A**?

Sometimes a single image of a cultural leader can tell a story. The portrait in **B** is a

 Artist unknown. (Detail) *Queen Tiy from the Tomb of Userhat,* 18th dynasty. Limestone relief, 16¾ by 15½ inches. Courtesy of Musées Royaux d'Art et d'Histoire, Brussels, Belgium.

Lesson 16

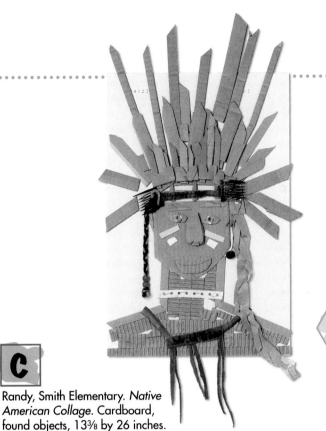

Randy, Smith Elementary. *Native American Collage.* Cardboard, found objects, 13⅜ by 26 inches.

Randy, Smith Elementary. *Native American Relief Sculpture.* Foil over cardboard collage, 13⅜ by 26 inches.

relief sculpture, or raised sculpture. This means that parts of it stand out from the background. Study details in **B** and read the credit line. What do they tell you about this queen who lived long ago? How could you find out more information to add to your story?

Try Your Hand

Making a Relief Sculpture

1. Read about a culture in history. Make a sketch of someone from that culture.
2. Assemble a collage-like portrait using recycled cardboard and other found objects. Cut and paste shapes to match your sketch.
3. Glue on layers of cardboard details. Let the portrait dry.
4. Brush the whole surface with thin, white glue.
5. Press a smooth sheet of aluminum foil over the cardboard portrait. Gently press with your fingers from the center outward.

Folk Art, Forms, and Functions

The artworks on these pages belong to a style called **Folk Art. Folk artists** are self-taught. They learn to make art by trying out their own ideas. Sometimes they learn by watching friends and family create artworks, too. Folk artists may whittle, carve, assemble, paint, build, or sculpt simply because they like to. They get pleasure from creating and imagining. Folk Art is often created for the artist's own use. It is commonly intended for home decoration and use.

The Folk artist of **A** worked in a toy factory before he began to make folk art. Notice the patterns on his playful sculpture. How would you describe the texture? Examine the credit line for sizes of the three dimensions. Based on this information, where would you suggest displaying the butterfly sculpture?

Gregorio Marzán. *Striped Butterfly,* ca. 1980s. Mixed media, 21 by 22½ by 6 inches. Collection El Museo del Barrio, New York. © Gregorio Marzán.

The Folk Art in **B** is from a country in Asia. The artist used unusual proportions to help create the mood of the artwork. How would you describe the mood of **B**?

The medium of **B** is **papier-mâché** (PAY-pur muh-SHAY). First, the artist made a stiff support, or **armature.** It is now inside the sculpture. The armature is often made of wire, cardboard, or wads of newspaper. It can even be an inflated balloon.

Next, the artist built up the form with strips of paper dipped in a watery paste. As each layer of paper strips dried, the form became stiff and hard. Finally, the artist decorated the form with paint and other objects.

When you look at **A** and **B**, you probably see positive space. The positive space is the part of the artwork that stands out from the background. Most people notice the positive space first. In each of these artworks, it is the sculpture itself. In **A** and **B**, the negative space is the background to each sculpture. Point out the positive and negative spaces in both **A** and **B**.

Artist unknown, Burma. *Doll,* ca. 1960. Painted papier-mache, height 10 inches. From the Girard Foundation Collection in the Museum of International Folk Art, a unit of the Museum of New Mexico, Santa Fe, NM. Photograph by Michael Monteaux.

Folk Art, Forms, and Functions 117

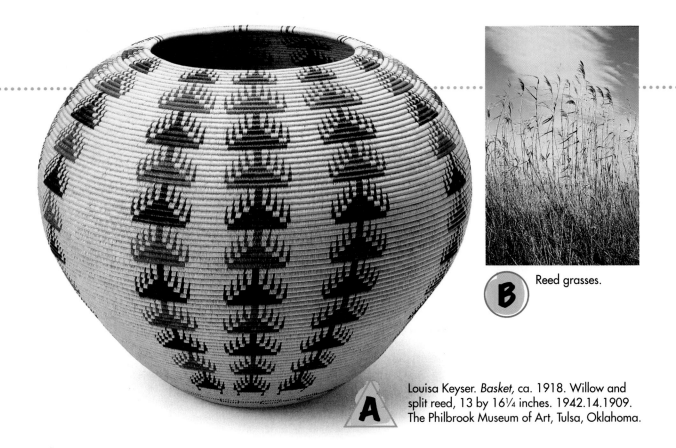

B Reed grasses.

A Louisa Keyser. *Basket*, ca. 1918. Willow and split reed, 13 by 16¼ inches. 1942.14.1909. The Philbrook Museum of Art, Tulsa, Oklahoma.

Fiber Arts

A **craftsperson** is an artist who has become highly skilled at making artworks by hand. Most craftspeople have received training in a certain medium. Their **craft** is usually their career. Often the **crafts** the artist makes are useful or are created for a special purpose. Many crafts are made to be sold. Some examples are ceramics, jewelry, fiber arts, mosaics, and furniture.

Louisa Keyser, also known as Dat So La Lee, was the skilled basketmaker of **A**. She was a member of the Washoe cultural group in California. The women of this American Indian group made many kinds of baskets. They used a variety of nearby fibers such as reeds and grasses. Many of the baskets were woven so tightly they could hold water. They helped the Washoe carry items as they traveled, hunting and gathering food.

Look at the patterns of triangles woven vertically into the basket in **A**. Notice how Keyser increased their sizes to match the form of the basket. How does this design feature create visual rhythm?

Artist unknown, Nagano, Japan. *Horse,* ca. 1960. Wrapped fiber, height 7⅜ inches. From the Girard Foundation Collection in the Museum of International Folk Art, a unit of the Museum of New Mexico, Santa Fe, NM. Photograph by Michael Monteaux.

Meredith, Stone Oak Elementary. *Happy Horse.* Raffia on wire, 7⅞ by 4 by 6⅝ inches.

Both craftspeople and Folk artists work with fibers. The Folk Art in **D** used to be a religious symbol in Japan. Today that same symbol is used in Japan as a good luck charm. What design features in **D** create movement? Explain.

The Folk artist of **D** made an armature of natural fibers. Point out other natural fibers that are wrapped around the armature. How would you describe the texture of the sculpture? How does the sculpture make you feel? What would you name it? Explain why.

 Try Your Hand

Making a Fiber Sculpture

1. Make an armature of an animal. Bend, twist, and wrap wire to create the form you want.
2. Wrap your armature with dampened raffia.
3. Add details with buttons, ribbons, pipe cleaners, and other found objects. Attach them with glue, or tie them to your sculpture.

Decorate a corner or shelf with your Folk Art. What title will you give your fiber sculpture?

Folk Art, Forms, and Functions **119**

Murals and Mosaics

Malou Flato. (Detail) *Mural,* 1993. Hand-glazed ceramic tiles, 3 panels, each 4½ by 21½ feet. Interior of Central Market grocery store in Austin, Texas. Photograph by Andrew Yates.

A **mural** is a large picture that decorates a surface such as a wall or a ceiling. One person or many people can create a mural. Often an artist designs the mural. Other people help by painting or assembling parts for it.

Muralists use different kinds of materials to make murals. Some artists paint directly onto the wall or ceiling. Others paint onto small tiles. The tiles are then attached to a wall or ceiling.

The artist in **A** designed and painted a mural for an interior wall of a grocery store. What is the mural about? Why do you suppose the muralist chose this theme for her mural? What story might you tell about this mural?

Notice the glassy texture of **A**. Locate the square clay tiles. The artist painted each tile with

Malou Flato.

special **glazes,** or minerals that stick to clay when they are fired. The fired glazes made the surface of the tiles appear shiny. Other people helped the artist attach the glazed tiles to the grocery-store wall.

Murals appear on the walls and ceilings of many buildings around the world. Some murals are old. Others are new. They each tell a story about a special culture.

Seeing, Planning, Thinking Like an Artist

1. Plan with your friends how to make a mural.
2. Agree upon a theme.
3. Make some sketches.

Murals and Mosaics

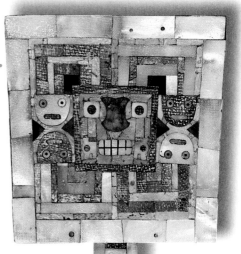

 Artist unknown. *The Court of Empress Theodora,* 547 A.D. Early Christian mosaic. S. Vitale, Ravenna, Italy. Photograph by Scala/Art Resource, New York.

 Artist unknown, Central or South coast of Peru. *Mirror,* 650–800 A.D. Mosaic of turquoise, pyrites, and shell, 9½ by 4¾ by ¾ inches. Dumbarton Oaks Research Library and Collections, Washington, D.C.

Mosaics Then and Now

Craftspeople have made **mosaics** for thousands of years. A mosaic is an artwork somewhat like a puzzle. It is made by fitting together small pieces of colored objects such as tile, glass, stone, or paper. These **tesserae** (TEH-sur-ray) often have small spaces between them.

In some buildings around the world, entire walls and floors are mosaics. The detail of one such mosaic in **A** shows a part of a mural on a wall in Italy. How can you tell that the woman is a member of a royal family? Point out different tesserae that show clothing and jewelry. Name two types of balance in the detail. Discuss the proportions of the facial features. Which lines, shapes, and colors emphasize the face?

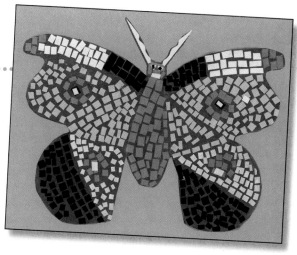

C Kristi, North Springs Elementary. *Cool Sun.* Construction-paper mosaic, 17¼ by 17½ inches.

D Salvador, Hogg Elementary. *Mosaic Butterfly.* Construction-paper mosaic, 24 by 18 inches.

The mosaic mirror in **B** was made long ago in South America. Read the credit line to discover the date. It shows a time before Christopher Columbus and other Europeans arrived in the Americas. This mirror and many other artworks were made before 1492. Why do you suppose such artworks are called **pre-Columbian**?

Pre-Columbian artworks were created in South America, Central America, and North America. Some of them can still be viewed in museums around the world. Other examples, such as pyramids and pictographs, remain in their natural settings. Pre-Columbian art gives clues and tells stories about the first people in the Americas.

Try Your Hand
Making a Mosaic

1. Choose a type of mosaic to make. Will it be a picture to frame? Could you decorate the frame of a mirror with tesserae? You could use paper, tile, stones, costume-jewelry pieces, and shells.
2. Study the guidelines on page 140 to help you make your mosaic.
3. Remember to work from the center of your mosaic outward. This will help you fit the tessarae together.

ARTIST AT WORK

David Bates
(1952–   )

David Bates and his dog Clovis.

Sometimes artist David Bates visits the junkyards near his studio. He sifts through strands of wire. He finds lumber that is almost 100 years old. Bates uses these objects to make sculptures. If you looked at one of these artworks, you would see an ordinary scene. You might see a dog or a man with a hat. But you would see these common objects in a new way.

Bates has not always been a sculptor. His early artworks are paintings. He first painted scenes, such as cowboys and roadside stands, from his Texas home. Then he saw Grassy Lake in Arkansas. To the artist, this wildlife preserve was "like a dream, a place of strange beauty." Snakes, birds, and fish appeared on his canvases. He painted images of men and women fishing and people he met. It was during this time that he painted *The Whittler* (page 110).

After Bates began creating sculpture, he said, "In painting, there's just a white canvas to start with, but an old block of wood can be a hand, or a pants cuff, or a foot." If you could visit an art exhibition of Bates's artworks today, you might see both paintings and sculptures. While you view his work, Bates might be looking for an old piece of wood at the junkyard.

WRITE ABOUT ART

A Word About
The Whittler

This modern painting shows a Folk artist sitting on his porch whittling, or carving, a stick. His dog rests at the whittler's feet. The mood of the portrait is happy and relaxed. Can you detect a hint of humor through the painter's use of details?

Look at *The Whittler*. Do you think that the man likes to whittle? How can you tell?

People often do things they enjoy, such as whittling, to feel relaxed and happy. Think of something that you enjoy doing. Do you like to ride a bike? Maybe you like to paint pictures. Perhaps you read a book or play soccer when you want to relax.

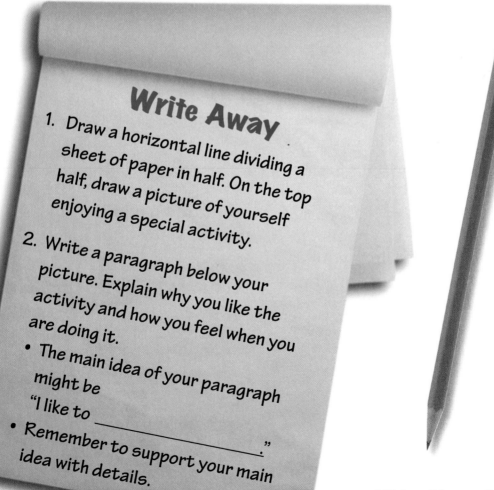

Write Away

1. Draw a horizontal line dividing a sheet of paper in half. On the top half, draw a picture of yourself enjoying a special activity.

2. Write a paragraph below your picture. Explain why you like the activity and how you feel when you are doing it.
   - The main idea of your paragraph might be "I like to _____."
   - Remember to support your main idea with details.

TALK ABOUT ART

David Bates. *The Whittler,* 1983. Oil on canvas, 96 by 78 inches. Archer M. Huntington Art Gallery, The University of Texas at Austin, Michener Collection Acquisition Fund, 1983. © David Bates. Photograph by George Holmes.

Look at A to answer these questions:

1. What do you see? List everything you see on the porch. Name the variety of lines you see. Describe the textures in the painting. Point out different patterns.

2. How is *The Whittler* arranged? How does the painter guide your eye to the knife and stick? Discuss the proportions of the whittler's face, arms, and feet. How did the painter show unity?

3. What does *The Whittler* mean? Why do you think the whittler is shown wearing black and white clothes? Explain why the painter included the dog. How does the painter's style add humor to the composition? What do you think the painter intended to say?

4. What's your opinion?

If you could meet the whittler in **A**, what questions would you ask him? Do you have a family member or friend who might like to see this painting? Explain. Have your feelings about the painting changed since you first saw it? Explain.

B Judith Leyster. *Self-Portrait,* ca. 1630. Oil on canvas, 29⅜ by 25⅝ inches. National Gallery of Art, Washington, D.C. Gift of Mr. and Mrs. Robert Woods Bliss. Photograph by Lorene Emerson.

Compare A and B.

How do the styles show that one painting is new and the other is old? Discuss what types of artists the subjects are. How did each painter emphasize the artist's tools? Point out other people, animals, and objects in each painting.

A Word About
Self-Portrait

Judith Leyster painted this self-portrait more than 350 years ago. Her realistic style shows a lively and natural pose. She was especially fascinated by the different ways that light shone on her subjects. Point out places in this painting that show her interest in lighting.

Making Forms with Papier-Mâché

What are the three dimensions of form?
How can you show them in a papier-mâché artwork?
Which form will you choose to show?

1. Choose an animal or another form for your subject. Begin to make an armature. Use cardboard tubes, wads of newspaper, wire, or an inflated balloon.

2. Tape details to your armature. Make weak parts stronger.

3. Dip 2-inch strips of newspaper into a tub of wallpaper paste. Run the strip through your fingers to squeeze away most of the paste.

4. Apply one layer of strips to your armature. Crisscross them as you go. Let the layer dry. Repeat with one or two more layers.

5. Paint the new form with tempera.

6. Add details with glue or yarn.

What title will you give your papier-mâché form?
Does it look real, imaginary, or both? Explain.
How does it make you feel?

Teresa, Hogg Elementary. *Up, Up, and Away!* Papier-mâché, tempera paint, felt, craft sticks, pipe cleaners, yarn, diameter 12 inches, height 28¼ inches.

Ernesto, Smith Elementary. *Chicken Little.* Papier-mâché, tempera paint, construction paper, 11⅜ by 12½ by 10¼ inches, including base.

What Have You Learned?

Sketchbook Progress

1. What themes for the mural did you and your friends discuss? What theme did you decide to use?

2. How did the theme help you to plan the mural?

3. Where will you hang your mural?

4. What materials and tools will you need to make the mural?

5. List the steps that you and your friends followed to plan a mural for the store.

Portfolio Progress

Try Your Hand

6. What person did you show in your relief sculpture? What details did you add?

7. Describe the details you added to your fiber sculpture. How does the title tell something you wanted to express?

8. Write down the steps you took to create your mosaic.

Portfolio Project

9. Measure your finished sculpture. Record the three dimensions of height, width, and depth.

10. Write a short story about your subject.

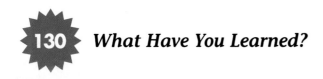

Unit Review

Diego, Smith Elementary.
Glue-Line Mask. Colored glue,
tempera on paper, approximately 8⅝ by 16½ inches.

1. Describe the shapes in the mask above. Has the artist used rhythm? Where?

2. Write some words that describe the expression on the mask.

3. What purpose might this mask serve in a culture?

4. What do you think would be a good name for this mask? Why?

5. What are some crafts you learned about in this unit?

6. Think about a mural that would be good for your school. What would you want the mural to be about?

Many Kinds of Art and Artists

Think Safety

Read these safety rules. Be sure to follow these rules when you create artworks.

1. **Keep art materials away from your face, especially your mouth and eyes.**

2. **Do not breathe chalk dust or art sprays.**

3. **If an art material makes you feel sick, tell your teacher right away.**

4. **Read the labels on art materials. Look for the word nontoxic on labels. This tells you the materials are safe to use.**

5. **Use safety scissors instead of scissors with sharp points. If you use a sharp object, point it away from your body.**

6. **Use only new meat trays and egg cartons.**

7. **Clean up after you finish an artwork. First, wash your hands with soap and water. Then wash tools you want to save, such as paintbrushes. Return art materials to their proper places.**

8. **If you have a problem with any art materials, ask your teacher for help.**

Can you think of more ways to be safe?

Guide to Using Art Tools and Media

Look at the pictures and read the instructions to learn more about using art tools and media. Review these pages if you need help when you create artworks.

Drawing with Crayons and Oil Pastels

1. Use the tip of a crayon or an oil pastel to make thin lines.

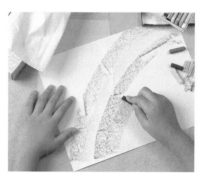

2. To make thick lines, peel the paper off the crayon or oil pastel. Then draw thick lines with the side. You may want to break the tool in half. This will keep your lines from being too thick.

3. When you use an oil pastel, press down firmly for a bright color. Press lightly for a softer color. Mix colors by putting one on top of another. Or, blend two colors with your fingers. Be sure to wipe the color from your fingers on a tissue before you go back to work.

Using Glue

1. Cover your work area with newspaper. Decide where you want to glue the item before you begin. Move the item around to find just the right spot.

2. Place the item you are gluing face down on the newspaper. Then put a small amount of glue in the center. Too much glue will cause the paper to wrinkle. Spread the glue in several places with your finger or with a glue brush. Spread glue on the edges and the corners.

3. Review where you want to place the item. Carefully lift it and place the glued side onto the surface to which you are gluing it. Lay clean paper on top of the item. Gently rub the paper with the palm of your hand.

Painting

Using a Paintbrush

1. Dip the bristles of your paintbrush into the paint. Push down on the paintbrush for thick lines. Be careful not to spread the bristles. Use the tip for thin lines. Try holding the brush at different angles when you paint. Remember to wear an art smock to keep your clothes clean.

2. Clean your paintbrush every time you switch colors. Dip the brush in water until it is clean. Wipe it on the side of the water container. Blot the brush on a paper towel. Move to your next color.

3. Wash your paintbrush when you have finished painting. Use warm, soapy water. Then rinse it. Blot the paintbrush on a towel. Put the paintbrush into a jar, bristles up.

Mixing Colors with Tempera Paint

1. To mix a tint, put some white paint on your tray. Add a small dot of colored paint and mix the two together. Keep adding very small amounts of color until you get the tint you want.

2. To mix a shade, start with a color. Add a small dot of black paint and mix the two together. Keep adding very small amounts of black until you get the shade you want. Be careful not to use too much black.

3. Try making these colors: Gray—Start with white and add a dot of black. Orange—Start with yellow and add a dot of red. Green—Start with yellow and add a dot of blue. Violet—Start with red and add a dot of blue. Brown—Start with red and add a dot of green. Make tints of orange, green, violet, and brown, too.

Making Prints

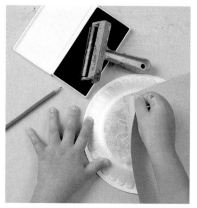

1. To make a monoprint, cover a sheet of paper or a hard, slick surface with paint. Use your finger or another tool to draw a design into the paint. Place a sheet of clean paper on top of your design. Smooth it down gently with your hands. Carefully peel the paper off. Let the paint dry.

2. To make a stamp print, cut a shape from material such as cardboard or a clean meat tray. Attach twisted masking tape to the back for a handle. Dip the face of the printing block in paint. Carefully, but firmly, press the block onto a piece of paper. Lift to see the print.

3. To make a relief print, use a pencil to draw a design on material such as a flattened piece of clay or a clean meat tray. Cover a roller, or brayer, with water-based printers' ink. Then roll the ink evenly over your design. Place a clean sheet of paper on top of your design. Rub the paper gently with your hands. Carefully pull the paper off your design. Let the ink dry.

Making a Collage

1. Decide on an idea for your collage. Will it show shape and color? Will it contain photographs? Then collect what you will need. Cut out shapes of colored paper or photographs from old magazines.

2. Select shapes, colors, and pictures that go well together. They might be shapes in warm or cool colors. They might be pictures of related subjects, such as foods, people, or animals.

3. Arrange your cutouts on a piece of construction paper. Move them around until you find an arrangement you like. Be sure you cover all parts of the paper. Glue the cutouts, one at a time, to the background. Use only a small amount of glue or your collage will wrinkle.

Working with Clay: Setting Up

1. Cover your desk or work area with a plastic mat, brown paper, or canvas. Gather the materials you will need:
- a lump of clay
- tools for carving
- found objects for pressing texture and designs into the clay
- a piece of cardboard to put your sculpture on
- a bowl of water

2. Prepare your clay by wedging it. Take a large lump of clay and thump it down on the work surface. Press into it with the palms of your hands. Turn the clay and press into it again. Keep turning and pressing until the clay has no more air bubbles in it.

3. Practice connecting clay parts by scoring them. Press a plastic fork onto the connecting points. Add slip, or water-thinned clay, to stick them together. You may keep slip in the bottom of your water bowl.

Using Found Objects in an Artwork

Be on the lookout for found objects you can use in artworks. They might be objects people throw away, such as cardboard tubes, milk cartons, and old buttons. Or, they might be things people don't use any more: keys, old jewelry, and bolts.

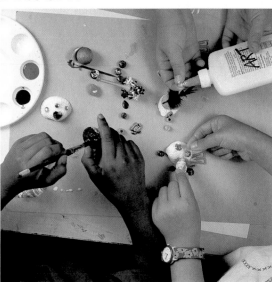

You can also find objects in nature, such as shells, sticks, rocks. You can put found objects together to make a sculpture.

Making a Clay Sculpture

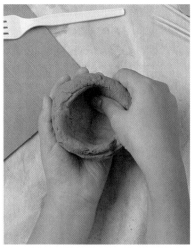

1. Make a clay sculpture by carving. Place a lump of clay on your desk or table. Flatten it with your hand. Use a plastic knife to cut shapes from the clay. Then join the shapes together. You can also carve shapes into the clay. Use drawing tools or found objects to make designs.

2. Make a clay sculpture by pinching. First, make a ball of clay. Roll a lump of clay between your hands. Then press your thumb into the middle of the ball. Pinch it with your fingers. Start pinching at the bottom and then move up and out. Keep turning the ball while you pinch.

3. May a clay sculpture by coiling. First, make a rope out of clay. Roll a lump of clay back and forth between your hands and the work surface. Start in the middle, then move out toward the edges. Keep rolling until the rope is the size you want it. You can coil the rope into a form. You can stack several ropes and shape them. You can cut coils into pieces and press them onto other clay shapes.

First plan a pleasing arrangement. Then tape and glue the parts together. You can paint your finished sculpture with tempera paint that has been mixed with a small amount of white glue. The glue will help the paint stick to some objects.

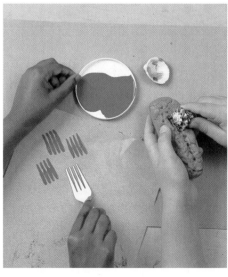

• You can make a print using found objects. Dip the face of the object in paint. Then press it onto your paper. Continue with one or more objects until you have made a pleasing design.
• You can create texture and designs on a clay sculpture with found objects. Press the object into the clay and then remove it. Repeat with other objects until you like the way your sculpture looks.

Portfolios **137**

Weaving

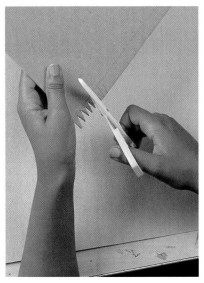

1. Make a loom to weave on. Cut a piece of cardboard the size you want your loom to be. Use a ruler to draw lines 1/2 inch from the top and from the bottom. Then make a mark every 1/4 inch or so along the lines. Draw slanted lines from the edge of the cardboard to the marks. Then cut along the slanted lines to make "teeth."

2. First, create a warp. Make a loop in one end of a piece of yarn. Hook the loop around the first "tooth" at the top of the loom.

Stitchery

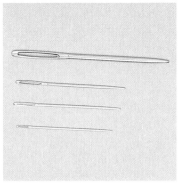

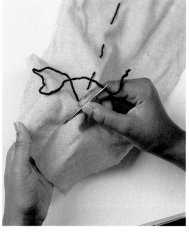

1. Artists use different kinds of needles and threads. A crewel needle is short and has a long eye. It is used for embroidery. A blunt needle is a big needle with a dull point. It can be used for weaving. A darner is a long needle with a big eye. It is used with thick thread like yarn. WARNING: Never use a sharp needle without the help of an adult.

2. To thread a needle, cut off a long piece of thread. Dampen your fingers and pinch the end of the thread together between them. This flattens the thread. Push the flattened end through the eye of the needle and pull it through. Make a knot at the other end to keep the thread from coming through the cloth.

3. Start a stitch on the back of the cloth. Push the needle through. Then pull the thread up until the knot stops it. Continue pushing and pulling the needle until you have finished your stitching. Finally, push the needle and thread through to the back. Make two small stitches next to each other. Push the needle under these two stitches. Pull thread through, knot it, and cut it off.

Then take the yarn down to the bottom of the loom. Hook it around the first "tooth" there. Take the yarn back up to the second "tooth" at the top, hook it, and so on. Keep wrapping until the loom is filled with vertical lines of yarn.

3. Next, weave the weft. Tie yarn through a hole in a narrow craftstick. Start at the bottom center of the loom. Weave toward one edge by going over and under the yarn. When you get to the last yarn, loop the craftstick around it and start weaving back in the

other direction. Keep weaving, over and under, until the loom is covered. Unhook and remove the weaving from the loom. Tie any loose end pieces.

Making a Sketchbook

1. Fold eight sheets of drawing paper in half. Make the top edges of the paper meet the bottom edges. Staple the sheets together along the fold. Take special care when you use a stapler. Keep your fingers away from the staple-press area.

2. Choose a color of construction paper. Fold it over your pages to make a cover. Carefully, staple it along the fold. Make sure it is connected to your pages.

3. Decorate your cover. Make drawings with crayons or markers. Glue on construction-paper shapes or pictures from magazines. Write your name on your sketchbook.

Making a Portfolio

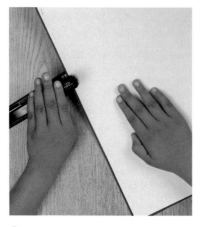

1. Place one sheet of poster board or heavy paper on top of another. Or fold a large piece of posterboard in half.

2. Staple or tape three sides together. Leave one long side open.

3. Decorate your portfolio. Use crayons, markers, or tempera paint. Or you may want to cut and paste shapes or pictures on your portfolio. Use your imagination! Be sure to write your name on your portfolio.

Making a Mosaic

1. Select and gather the tesserae for your mosaic. You can use small pieces of colored paper or tile. Or you might choose small stones, beads, or shell. Small pieces of shell or tile can have sharp edges. Take care when you handle these.

2. Draw the shape for your mosaic on a base. The base can be made of heavy paper, wood, cardboard, or an item you want to decorate.

3. Paint a small area in the center of your base with the glue. Working outward from the center, glue pieces of tesserae to the base. Leave a small amount of space around each piece. Add more glue to the base as you need it. Continue in this way until you have covered the shape with tesserae.

Glossary

abstract (AB-strakt) A style of art that is not realistic. Abstract art usually contains geometric shapes, bold colors, and lines.

actual Something that is real, not imaginary.

analogous colors (uh-NAL-uh-gus) Colors that appear next to each other on the color wheel. Analagous colors have one hue in common. For example, blue, blue-green, and blue-red all contain blue. Also called related colors.

animator A person who creates animation.

animation (an-ah-MAY-shun) The art of putting together drawings in a sequence. The pictures are recorded onto film or tape. When the film is run at high speed, the pictures appear to be in motion.

appliqué (AP-li-KAY) An artwork created by sewing small pieces of cloth onto a larger cloth background.

arch A curved shape in a building. An arch can frame a doorway or it can support a wall or ceiling.

architect (AR-kih-tekt) A person who designs buildings and supervises the building process.

architecture (AR-kih-tek-chur) The art and science of designing buildings and other structures.

armature (ARM-uh-chur) A frame made of wire or other materials and around which a sculpture can be formed.

art center A group of buildings that relate to art. They may include an art museum, a theater for performing arts, a fine-arts library, a music building, and a dance studio.

art criticism (KRIT-uh-siz-um) The process of looking at, thinking about, and judging an artwork.

art history The study of art created in different times and cultures.

art media The materials used by artists.

assemblage (uh-SEM-blej) A three-dimensional work of art made by joining objects together.

asymmetrical balance (ay-sih-MEH-tri-kul BAL-uns) A type of balance in which the two sides of an artwork look equally important even though they are not alike.

background The part of an artwork that seems the farthest away.

balance The way an artwork is arranged to make different parts seem equally important. Balance is a principle of design.

batik (bah-TEEK) An art form in which dye and wax are used to make pictures or patterns on cloth.

blend To mix or rub colors together.

block In printmaking, a piece of flat material, such as wood or metal, with a design on the surface. The block is used to print the design. (See also plate.) In sculpture, a solid material, such as wood or stone, used for carving.

blueprint A plan for building something. It is usually printed with white lines on a blue background.

border A framelike edge around a shape or image.

brayer (BRAY-ur) In printing, a rubber roller used to spread ink over a surface.

brush stroke A line, shape, mark, or texture made with a paintbrush.

camera An instrument used to take photographs.

canvas A strong, closely woven fabric, often used as a surface for painting.

career A person's job or profession.

caricature (KAIR-ik-uh-chur) An artwork that exaggerates the features or aspects of a person or object, usually in a way that is funny.

cartoon An artwork that shows people or things in ways that are funny. Cartoons often have words that go with them.

carve To cut away parts from a block of wood, stone, or other hard material.

center of interest The part of an artwork that you notice first.

ceramics (sir-AM-iks) The art of making objects from clay and hardening them with fire. Also artworks made by this process.

cityscape Artwork that gives a view of a city.

clay A soft, moist material used to create artworks such as sculpture and pottery.

close-up A very near or close view of something.

coil A rope-like shape that has been rolled from clay or other such material. Pottery and sculpture are often made of coils.

collage (kuh-LAZH) Artwork made by gluing bits of paper, pictures, fabric, or other materials to a flat surface.

color family A group of related colors. For example, warm colors and cool colors are color families.

color scheme (skeem) A plan for combining colors in a work of art.

color wheel Colors arranged in a certain order in the shape of a circle.

complementary (kom-pluh-MEN-ter-ee) **colors** Colors that contrast with one another. Complementary colors are opposite one another on the color wheel.

compose To design or create something by arranging different parts into a whole.

computer-aided animation Animation, or moving pictures, created with the help of a computer.

construct To make something by putting together materials.

contour The outline of a shape.

contrast The effect of showing the difference between two unlike things, such as a dark color and a light color.

contrasting colors Colors placed opposite one another on the color wheel. Also called complementary colors. For example, orange and blue are contrasting colors.

cool colors The family of colors that includes greens, blues, and violets. Cool colors bring to mind cool things, places, and feelings.

craft An artist's skill in creating things.

craftsworker An artist who creates handicrafts.

crayon etching (EH-ching) A picture made by rubbing wax crayon onto paper and then scratching a design into the wax.

creative Having a skill or talent for making things in a new or different way.

credit line The information that is given with a picture of an artwork. A credit line usually tells the artist, title, date, medium, size, and location of an artwork.

cultural style A style of art that shows something about the culture in which the artist lives or lived.

culture The customs, beliefs, arts, and way of life of a group of people.

decorative arts Handicrafts that result in a beautiful, useful object. Rug and fabric design, furniture-making, and glassblowing are all decorative arts.

decorative Artworks that give visual pleasure.

design A plan for the arrangement of lines, spaces, colors, shapes, and textures in an artwork. Also, the act of arranging the parts of an artwork.

detail A small part of an artwork.

diagonal A slanted edge or line.

distance The sense of depth or space between objects in an artwork. (*See* perspective.)

docent (DOH-sent) A person who volunteers in an art museum. Docents give information and conduct tours.

dye A colored liquid used to stain fabric.

earthwork A sculptural form made of natural materials, such as soil, rocks, or plants.

easel (EEZ-ul) A stand with three legs, used to hold a painting while an artist works on it.

edge The outside line of a shape or form.

editorial cartoon Cartoons that make a statement about something that is happening in the news.

editorial cartoonist An artist who creates editorial cartoons.

elements of art The basic parts of an artwork. Line, color, value, shape, texture, form, and space are elements of art.

emphasis (EM-fuh-sis) Importance given to certain objects or areas in an artwork. Color, texture, shape, and size can be used to create emphasis. Emphasis is a principle of design.

engrave To use sharp tools to carve letters or pictures into a metal, wood, or other hard surfaces. Also called etching.

enlargement A copy of a picture that is larger than the original.

exaggeration (egg-ZADJ-uhr-RAY-shun) Showing something is a way that makes it seem larger or more important than it is.

expression (ex-SPRESH-un) A special look that communicates a feeling. A smile is an expression of happiness.

Expressionists A group of artists who use simple designs and brilliant colors to express feelings. Artists began Using this style in Germany in the early 1900s. It gained interest in the United States in the 1940s and 1950s..

expressive (ek-SPRESS-iv) Showing strong feelings.

exterior (ek-STEER-ee-ur) The outer part of a building or other form.

eye-dazzler blanket A type of blanket in which bold colors and patterns are used to delight or surprise the viewer.

fabric Cloth made by knitting or weaving threads together.

fantasy Something that reflects the imaginary.

femmage A special type of collage that includes fabric art traditionally made by women.

fiber artist An artist who creates artworks by sewing, weaving, knitting, or stitching fibers together.

fibers The threads that make up yarn, string, fabric, and other such materials.

film A thin strip of material used in a camera. Images are captured on film and then developed into pictures.

filmmaking The artistic process of creating motion pictures.

fired Hardened by great heat. Clay objects are sometimes fired to make ceramics.

firing The process of using extreme heat, such as putting clay objects in a kiln.

floorplan The arrangement of rooms in a building.

flip book A book in which each page shows a part of an action. When the pages are flipped, the viewer sees an animated sequence.

Folk art Art made by people who have not been formally trained in art. Folk art usually reflects the artist's culture or tradition.

Folk artist An artist who creates Folk art.

foreground The part of an artwork that seems nearest.

form A three-dimensional object, such as a cube or a ball. Form is an element of art.

found object Something that an artist finds and uses in an artwork. A scrap of metal or a piece of wood could be a found object.

frame One of many pictures in a filmstrip. Also a decorative border or support for an artwork.

frontal view In an artwork a view of the front side of an object or person.

functional Designed with a special purpose in mind.

galleries Places where artwork can be seen and bought.

glaze A thin, transparent, glassy coating on ceramics.

geometric (jee-oh-MEH-trik) A word describing shapes and forms such as squares, circles, cubes, and spheres.

German Expressionism A style of art developed in Germany in the early 1900s. The German Expressionists used bright, bold colors and expressed feelings in their artworks.

graphic (GRAF-ik) **design** The design of commercial art, such as signs, posters, book jackets, and advertisements.

graphic designer Someone who creates commercial art.

heritage The history, culture, and traditions of a group of people.

horizon line In an artwork, the line where the ground and sky meet.

horizontal Moving straight across from side to side rather than up-and-down. For example, the top edge of a piece of paper is horizontal.

hue (hyoo) Another word for color.

ideal Something in its perfect or most beautiful form.

illusion (ih-LOO-zhun) An image that tricks the eye or seems to be something it is not.

illustration (ih-luh-STRAY-shun) A picture used to help explain something or tell a story.

illustrator An artist who creates pictures for books, magazines, or other printed works.

imagination A mental picture of something that may or may not exist.

implied Suggested, but not actually shown.

Impressionists A group of artists in the late 19th and early 20th centuries who paid special attention to light and its effect on subjects in their paintings.

industrial (in-DUS-tree-ul) **design** The design of objects used or sold in industry, such as telephones and cars.

industrial designer An artist who helps design products people buy, such as hair dryers, telephones, and toasters.

interior (in-TEER-ee-ur) The inside of a building or another hollow form, such as a box.

interior (in-TEER-ee-ur) **design** The art of planning and creating indoor spaces such as rooms.

intermediate (in-tur-ME-dee-ut) **colors** Colors that are a mixture of a primary and a secondary color. Blue-green, red-orange, and red-violet are examples of intermediate colors.

kiln A very hot oven used to harden or dry a substance such as clay.

label Words that define, describe, or explain.

landscape A drawing or painting that shows outdoor scenery such as trees, lakes, mountains, and fields.

landscape architect A person who uses plants, rocks, trees, and other materials to create a pleasing outdoor designs.

line A thin mark on a surface created by a pen, pencil, or brush. Line is an element of art.

loom A frame or machine used to hold yarn or other fibers for weaving.

mask An artwork made to be placed over a person's face for decoration or disguise.

media (MEE-dee-uh) Materials used to create an artwork, such as clay or paint. The singular of media is medium.

middle ground In an artwork, the part between the foreground and the background.

miniature (MIN-ee-uh-chur) An artwork made in a very small size.

mixed media Artworks that are created from more than one medium.

model Someone or something an artists uses as an example when creating an artwork. Also a small copy of something.

monochrome (MON-oh-krome) A color scheme using only tints and shades of a single color.

monoprint A print made from a plate that can be used only once.

mood The feeling created in a work of art.

mosaic (moh-ZAY-ik) An artwork made from small pieces of colored glass, stone, paper, or other materials.

motion A sense of movement or action in an artwork.

motion picture An art form in which pictures are printed on a long strip of film. The film is then shown rapidly to give a sense of motion.

movement The sense of motion or action created in an artwork. Also, a trend in art is called a movement.

mural (MYOOR-ul) A large artwork, usually a painting, that is created or placed on a wall or ceiling, often in a public place.

muralist An artist who creates murals.

museum A place where works of art are cared for and displayed.

museum educators People who work in museums to help visitors explore artworks and art processes.

needlework Artworks that are created using fabric and some kind of stitchery.

negative space The empty space around and between forms or shapes in an artwork.

neutrals A word used for black, white, and tints and shades of gray. (Some artists use tints and shades of brown as neutrals.)

nonobjective A style of art that does not represent real objects.

oil paint A paint made from a mixture of colored pigment and special oil.

opaque (oh-PAKE) Not letting light through; the opposite of transparent.

organic A word describing shapes and forms similar to those in nature.

outline The line that forms the edge of any shape or form. Also called the contour.

pulled threadwork An artwork created by pulling threads from a piece of fabric in a way that creates a design.

overlap To partly or completely cover one shape or form with another.

palette (PAL-it) A flat board on which an artist holds and mixes colors.

papier-mâché (PAY-pur muh-SHAY) A process of creating forms by covering an armature or other base with strips of paper that have been soaked in watery paste, and then molding the strips. The form hardens as it dries.

pastel A crayon made of either chalk or oil.

pattern Repeated colors, lines, shapes, or textures in an artwork. Pattern is a principal of design. Also, a plan or model to be followed when making something.

perspective A way of making a flat artwork look as if it has depth. In a painting, an artist creates perspective by making far-away objects smaller and nearby objects larger.

photograph An image made by recording light on film and then printing the image on paper.

photography The art of taking pictures with a camera and film.

photomontage (FOH-toh-mon-TAZH) A picture made by combining parts of different photographs.

pictographs (PICK-toh-grafs) Ancient drawings, often found on cave walls, that tell stories or record a culture's beliefs and practices.

pinch method A way of shaping a ball of clay into pottery by pinching, pulling, and pressing it with the hands.

plate In printmaking, a piece of flat material, such as wood or metal, with a design on the surface. The plate is used to print the design. *(See also block.)*

portrait A work of art created to show a person, animal, or group of people, usually focusing on the face.

pose The way subjects sit or stand while an artist paints portraits of them.

positive space Shapes, forms, or lines that stand out from the background in a work of art.

potter An artist who makes pottery.

potter's wheel A flat, spinning disc used by potters. Potters place soft clay on a spinning wheel and then use their hands to shape the clay into a form.

pre-Columbian Artworks created in the Americas before Christopher Columbus and other Europeans arrived in the area.

primary colors The colors from which all other colors are made. The primary colors are red, yellow, and blue.

principles of design Guidelines that artists use as they create art works. Unity, variety, emphasis, balance, proportion, pattern, and rhythm are the principles of design.

print An artwork made by covering a textured object or a carved design with ink and then pressing it onto paper or pressing paper onto it.

printing block A block of wood or other hard material with a design carved into it. To print the design, the block is covered with ink and then paper is pressed onto it.

printmaker An artist who uses the art process of printmaking.

profile Something that is seen or shown from the side, such as a side view of a face.

prop In an artwork, an object held or used by the subject

proportion The size or placement of something in relation to another thing. Proportion is a principle of design.

pulled threadwork An artwork created by pulling threads from a piece of fabric in a way that creates a design.

quilt A decorative bedcover. Quilts are made by first sewing together two squares of cloth and stuffing the square with padding. Then squares are stitched together in a certain pattern.

quilt block A square, usually of fabric, that is decorated in some way and combined with others to create a quilt.

radial balance A type of balance in which lines or shapes spread out from a center point.

Realism A style of art in which artists attempt to show what they perceive through their senses.

realistic Showing something, such as a person or scene, as it might really look.

related colors Colors such as yellow, yellow-orange, and orange that are next to each other on the color wheel. Also called analogous colors.

relief print A print made by covering a printing block with ink and pressing paper onto the block.

relief sculpture A kind of sculpture in which a design or image is carved into a flat surface.

renovated (REN-oh-vay-ted) Remodeled or restored.

resist medium A material, such as wax, used to protect parts of a surface from paint or dye.

rhythm (RIH-thum) The repeating of elements, such as lines, shapes, or colors, that creates a pattern of visual motion in an artwork. Rhythm is a principle of design.

rubbing An artwork created by placing paper on a raised surface and then rubbing the paper with chalk, crayon, or a pencil.

sculpture An artwork made by modeling, carving, or joining materials into a three-dimensional form. Clay, wood, stone, and metal are often used to make sculptures.

seascape An artwork that includes in the scene the sea, ocean, or shore.

secondary colors A color made by mixing two primary colors. The secondary colors are green, violet, and orange.

self-portrait A drawing, painting, photograph, or sculpture that shows the likeness of the artist.

shade A color made by adding black to a hue. For example, adding black to green results in dark green. Also, a dark value of a color. (See value.)

shading A way of showing gradual changes in lightness or darkness in a drawing or painting. Shading helps make a picture look more realistic.

shape A flat area, such as a circle or a square, that has clear boundaries. Shape is an element of art.

sketch (skech) A quick drawing. A sketch can be used to explore or plan an artwork.

sketchbook A book or pad of paper used for drawing and keeping sketches.

space An empty surface or area. Also, the area surrounding something.

site-specific Refers to an artwork that must be viewed in a certain place. The place often is a part of the artwork.

still life An artwork showing an arrangement of objects that cannot move on their own, such as fruit or flowers.

still photographer Someone who takes photographs using a camera and film.

story quilt A quilt showing pictures that tell a story. (See quilt.)

studio A room or building where an artist creates art.

style An artist's own way of designing and creating art. Also, a technique used by a group of artists in a particular time or culture.

subject What an artwork is about. A person, animal, object, or scene can be the subject of an artwork.

subtractive A word describing sculpture that is made by taking away, or subtracting, material from a larger piece or block.

surface The outside layer of a material, an object, or another form.

symbol A letter, color, sign, or picture that expresses a larger meaning. For example, a red heart is often used as a symbol for love.

symmetrical (sih-MEH-tri-kul) **balance** A type of balance in which both sides of an artwork look the same or almost the same.

symmetry (SIH-muh-tree) Balance created by making both sides of an artwork the same or almost the same.

tactile A texture you can feel with your hands.

technique (tek-NEEK) The way an artist uses art materials to create a certain type of artwork.

technology The way human beings use machines and other tools to make or do something.

tempera paint A chalky, water-based paint. Also called poster paint.

tesserae (TEH-sur-ray) Small pieces of material, such as paper, stone, tile, or glass used to make a mosaic.

texture The way a surface looks and feels, such as smooth, rough, or bumpy. Texture is an element of art.

theme In an artwork, the artist's message about the subject of the work.

three-dimensional Having height, width, and thickness. Forms are three-dimensional.

tint A color such as pink that is created by mixing a hue with white. Also, a light value of a color. *(See value.)*

tradition Knowledge, beliefs, and activities handed down from one generation to the next.

unity (YOO-ni-tee) The quality of seeming whole and complete, with all parts looking right together. Unity is a principle of design.

value (VAL-yoo) The lightness or darkness of colors. Tints have a light value. Shades have a dark value. Value is an element of art.

variety (vuh-RY-ih-tee) The combination of elements of art, such as line, shape, or color, in an artwork. Variety is a principle of design.

vertical Moving up and down rather than side to side. For example, the side edge of a piece of paper is vertical.

videotape A film containing a series of pictures. When the pictures are shown at high speed, they give the sense of motion.

visual (VIH-zhoo-ul) **rhythm** In an artwork, rhythm created by repeating elements, such as colors and lines. Visual rhythm might remind a viewer of music or dance rhythm.

warm colors The family of colors that includes reds, yellows, and oranges. Warm colors bring to mind warm things, places, and feelings.

warp In weaving, the vertical threads attached to the top and bottom of a loom.

weaver An artist who creates weavings.

weaving An artwork made of thread, yarn, or other fibers laced or woven together on a loom.

weft The threads woven back and forth, over and under the warp fibers on a loom.

Elements of Art

Line

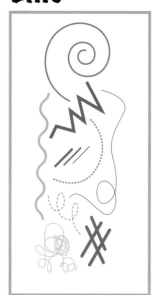

Color

Value

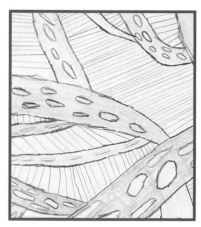

Texture

Form

Shape

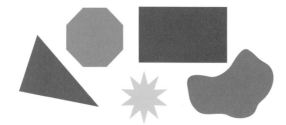

Space

Point out examples of the elements of art in the artwork below. Your glossary may help you recall their meanings.

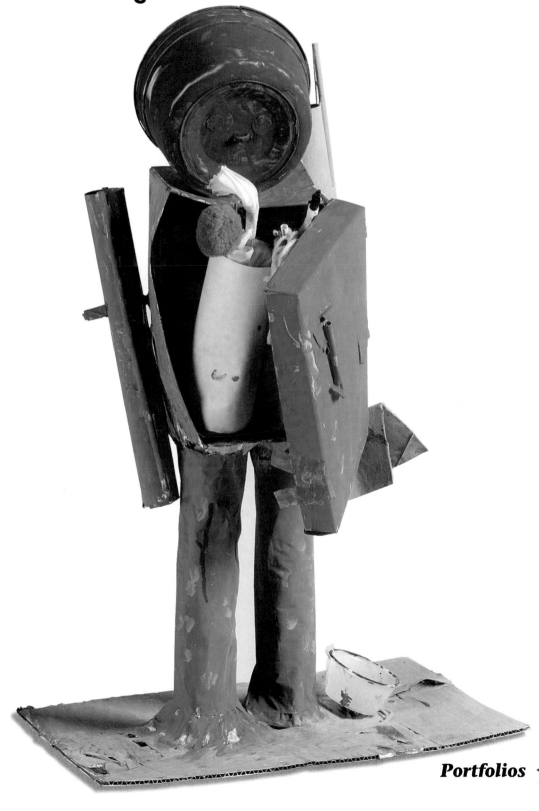

Principles of Design

Balance

Pattern

Rhythm

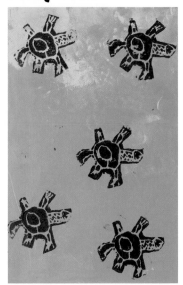

Variety

Unity

Proportion

Emphasis

Point out examples of the principles of design in the artwork below. Your glossary may help you recall their meanings.

Color Wheel

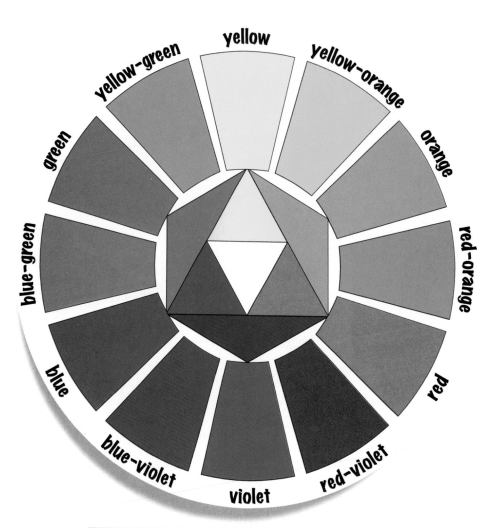

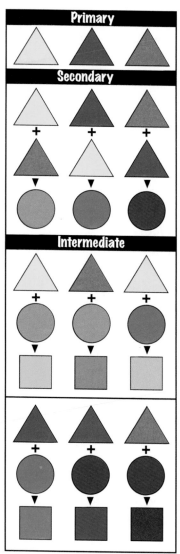

Point out and identify types of colors in the artwork. The chart above may help you identify types of color.

List of Art and Artists

Unknown Artists

Artists

Artworks

Index

ACKNOWLEDGMENTS

CONTRIBUTORS

The author and publisher wish to thank the following teachers for their contributions to the development of ideas and procedures for art activities and projects in this series:

Martha Camacho, Wanza Coates, Joan Elder, Kelly Fox, Lisa Fuentes, Maureen Clare Gillis, Karen Johnson, Joan Klasson, Leisa M. Koch, Lara Landers, Tamera S. Moore, Sharon R. Nagy, Teri Evans-Palmer, Julie Pohlmann, Jean Powell, Cynde Riddle, Nancy J. Sass, Lori Schimmel, Melissa St. John, Sue Telle, Susan Urband, Fatima Usrey, Pamela Valentine, Caryl E. Williams

We appreciate the efforts of the following teachers who graciously submitted student art for use in this series:

Wanza Coates, Linda Caitlin, Joan Elder, Kelly Fox, Karen Johnson, Joan Klasson, Dottie Myers, Julie Pohlmann, Jean Powell, Dana Reyna, Nancy J. Sass, Lori Schimmel, Ingrid Sherwood, Melissa St. John, Tammy Suarez, Marie Swope, Sue Telle, Susan Urband, Fatima Usrey, Jamie Woods, Marilyn Wylie.

We wish to thank the following teachers for their expertise, wisdom, and wholehearted good will during the field testing of this series:

Judy Abbott, Laurie Adams, Marti Fox, Sammie Gray, Joan Klasson, Mary Alice Lopez, Robin Maca, Deborah McLouth, April Money, Jennifer Owers, Lois Pendley, Dana Reyna, Ingrid Sherwood, Melissa St. John, Sue Telle, Pamela Valentine, Marilyn Wylie.

We gratefully acknowledge the following schools for allowing us to work with their teachers and students during the development of this series:

Conley Elementary, Aldine Independent School District; Roosevelt Elementary, San Antonio Independent School District; Amelia Earhart Learning Center, Dallas Independent School District; Cedar Creek Elementary, Eanes Independent School;Smith Elementary, Alief Independent School District; Heflin Elementary, Alief Independent School District; Hill Elementary, Austin Independent School District; Odom Elementary, Austin Independent School District; Brooke Elementary, Austin Independent School District; Campbell Elementary, Austin Independent School District; Zavala Elementary, Austin Independent School; Langford Elementary, Austin Independent School District; Brentwood Elementary, Austin Independent School District; Burnet Elementary, San Antonio Independent School District; Edgewater Elementary, Anne Arundel County Public Schools; Landis Elementary, Alief Independent School District; Boone Elementary, Alief Independent School; College of Fine Art, Maryland Institute, Baltimore, Maryland; Orange Grove Elementary, Aldine Independent School District; Klentzman Intermediate School, Alief Independent School District; Forest Trail Elementary, Eanes Independent School District; Teague Middle School, Teague Independent School District; Martin Elementary, Alief Independent School District; Petrosky Elementary, Alief Independent School District; North Hi Mount Elementary, Fort Worth Independent School District; Cambridge Elementary, Alamo Heights Independent School District; Porter Elementary, Birdville Independent School District; Woodridge Elementary, Alamo Heights Independent School District; Anderson Academy, Aldine Independent School District; Creative Fine Arts Magnet School, San Francisco Unified School District; Wonderland School, San Marcos, Texas; Olsen Park

Elementary, Amarillo Independent School District; Liestman Elementary, Alief Independent School District; Hogg Elementary, Dallas Independent School District; Bivins Elementary, Amarillo Independent School District; Tuckahoe Elementary, Arlington Public Schools, Fine Arts Department of North East Independent School District; Fox Hill Elementary, Indianapolis Public Schools; Eanes Elementary, Eanes Independent School District; Allison Elementary, Austin Independent School District; Collins Intermediate School, Conroe Independent School District; Bethune Academy, Aldine Independent School District; Loma Park Elementary, Edgewood Independent School District; Randolph Field Elementary, Randolph Field Independent School District; Brauchle Elementary, Northside Independent School District.

A special acknowledgment to the founders of the SHARE program in San Antonio, Texas, Pamela Valentine and Sue Telle, who graciously allowed us to share with the world their prized and inspirational student artwork. The SHARE (Students Help Art Reach Everyone) program is a foundation dedicated to students and their art, and develops opportunities for students to interact with and enlighten their community.

A final acknowledgment to Barrett and Kendall Blevins, the inspiration behind Portfolios.

PHOTO CREDITS

Key: (t) top, (c) center, (b) bottom, (l) left, (r) right.

UNIT 1.   Page 2(tl) Barrett Kendall photos by Andrew Yates; 4(br) Barrett Kendall photo by Andrew Yates; 5(tr) Barrett Kendall photo by Andrew Yates; 6(tr) © Stephen J. Krasemann/Photo Researchers; 6(cr) © Phil Jude/Science Photo Library/Photo Researchers; 6(br) © SuperStock.

UNIT 2.   Page 26(tl) © Robyn M. Turner; 27(cl) © Robyn M. Turner; 27(tr) © L. Padelsky/SuperStock; 29(t) © Robyn M. Turner.

UNIT 3.   Page 54(t) Zintgraff Collection, The Institute of Texan Cultures, San Antonio, Texas; 55(tl) © Tony Freeman/PhotoEdit; 55(tr) © SuperStock; 56(tl), 56(tr) Texas Department of Commerce/Tourism; 58(t) © Tracye Saar.

UNIT 4.   Page 73(tl) © 1971 Thomas Sennett/Magnum Photos, Inc.; 78(tl) Texas Department of Commerce/Tourism; 80(tr) Courtesy of Estate of Romare Bearden.

UNIT 5.   Page 92(tl) © Adam Woolfitt/Woodfin Camp & Associates; 93(tl) Barrett Kendall photo by Sharon Warwick; 95(tl) Courtesy of Ben Sargent.

UNIT 6.   Page 114(tr) Texas Department of Commerce/Tourism; 118(tr) Courtesy of Dr. E. R. Degginger; 120(br) Courtesy of Malou Flato; 124(tr) Photo by Lee Clockman, courtesy of Gerald Peters Gallery.

Pages 133-140, Barrett Kendall photos by Andrew Yates.

ILLUSTRATION CREDITS

Holly Cooper: 32, 33, 84, 101

David Fischer: 18, 40

Mike Krone: 49, 57, 62, 106, 128